Higher Education

in Portuguese Speaking African Countries

A FIVE COUNTRY BASELINE STUDY

Patrício Vitorino Langa

Published in 2013 by African Minds
4 Eccleston Place, Somerset West, 7130, South Africa
info@africanminds.org.za
www.africanminds.org.za

ISBN: 978-1-920677-03-9

 2013 Patrício Langa

For orders from within South Africa:
Blue Weaver
PO Box 30370, Tokai 7966, Cape Town, South Africa
Email: orders@blueweaver.co.za

For orders from outside South Africa:
African Books Collective
PO Box 721, Oxford OX1 9EN, UK
orders@africanbookscollective.com
www.africanbookscollective.com

Design and lay-out by COMPRESS.dsl | www.compressdsl.com

Published in collaboration with the Association for the Development of Education in Africa (ADEA).

The author of the study is responsible for the choice and presentation of the data and facts contained in this document and for the opinions expressed therein, and which are not necessarily those of ADEA nor the various individuals who were interviewed or provided data.

Contents

Tables

Figures

Acknowledgements

This research was funded by the Association for the Development of Education in Africa (ADEA) through its Working Group on Higher Education (WGHE). I am most indebted to officials from all the ministries of education in the Portuguese speaking countries in Africa (PALOP), who provided me with useful data, and university managers, who shared their ideas with me and gave me their time. I wish to express thanks to Prof. Arlindo Chilundo, Deputy Minister of Education, Mozambique and Ms Alice Sena Lamptey, Coordinator of ADEA's Working Group on Higher Education for their support.

I am also indebted to the following people, without whom this study would have not been possible:

Research assistants

Mrs Isabel Pinto (Angola)
Dr   Arlindo Mendes (Cape Verde)
Mr   Ivo de Barros (Guinea-Bissau)
Dr   Nelson Zavale (Mozambique)
Mr   Alex Afonso (São Tomé and Príncipe)

External academic reviewers

Dr   Gerald Wangenge-Ouma, University of the Western Cape, South Africa
Dr   Thierry Luescher-Mamashela, University of the Western Cape, South Africa

Acronyms and abbreviations

AAU	Association of African Universities
ADEA	Association for the Development of Education in Africa
CESD	Centro de Estudos de Ensino Superior e Desenvolvimento
CNAQ	Conselho Nacional de Avaliação de Qualidade do Ensino Superior, Mozambique
CNES	Conselho Nacional do Ensino Superior
EGUA	Estudos Gerais Universitários de Angola
EGUM	Estudos Gerais Universitários de Moçambique
FNLA	National Front for the Liberation of Angola
FRELIMO	Front of the Mozambican Liberation
GER	Gross enrolment rate
HDI	Human Development Index
HE	Higher education
HEI	Higher education institution
ICT	Information and communication technology
IMF	International Monetary Fund
ISCRSRI	Instituto Superior de Ciências Sociais e Relações Internacionais
ISDB	Instituto Superior Dom Bosco
ISJP II	Instituto Superior João Paulo II
ISPs	Internet Service Providers
IST	Instituto Superior Técnico
ISTA	Instituto Superior Técnico de Angola
JDZ	Joint Development Zone
MHESD	Masters Programme in Higher Education Studies and Development
MLSTP	Movement for the Liberation of São Tomé and Príncipe
MPLA	Movement for the Liberation of Angola
ODA	Overseas development assistance
PAIGC	African Party for the Independence of Guinea and Cape Verde
PALOP	Países Africanos de Língua Oficial Portuguesa (Portuguese speaking countries in Africa)
QA	Quality assurance

SEES	Secretaria de Estado do Ensino Superior
TDM	Mozambican Telecommunication Company
UAN	Universidade Agostinho Neto
UCA	Universidade Católica de Angola
UCT	University of Cape Town
UGS	Universidade Gregório Semedo
UJP	Universidade Jean Piaget de Angola
ULA	Universidade Lusíada de Angola
ULM	Universidade de Lourenço Marques
UNA	Universidade de Angola
UNB	Universidade de Belas
UNIA	Universidade Independente de Angola
UNI-CV	University of Cape Verde
UNITA	National Union for Total Independence of Angola
UNL	Universidade de Luanda
UNM	Universidade Metropolitana
UNMA	Universidade Metodista de Angola
UNPA	Universidade Privada de Angola
UOR	Universidade Óscar Ribas
UTA	Universidade Técnica de Angola
UWC	University of the Western Cape

Preface

When the Honourable Deputy Minister of Education of Mozambique, Prof. Arlindo Gonçalves Chilundo, proposed the idea of undertaking a study to map the state of higher education in the five Portuguese speaking countries in Africa (PALOP), ADEA readily accepted to commission and fund the study. This was in part in order to throw the spotlight on these five countries, to address those historically neglected from mainstream higher education research, advocacy and policy dialogue, and as part of ADEA and partners' efforts to address the challenges posed by the disparate higher education systems Africa inherited from its colonial – past namely Anglophone, Francophone and Lusophone higher education systems, with some Arab countries in North Africa having their own specific systems. This challenge, more than anything, handicaps the mobility of staff and students within the continent, and statistics show that academic mobility outwards from the continent by far exceeds that within.

As the evidence from this study shows, Africa, in particular sub-Saharan Africa, comprises some of the poorest nations in the world and therefore desperately needs strong higher education systems that can assist in its rapid development. It is widely acknowledged that higher education plays a key role in the economic, scientific, social and human development of any country, and that the economically strongest nations are those with the best performing higher education sectors. Higher education, as the producer of knowledge and knowledge workers, is assuming an even more important role with the realisation that knowledge, not natural resources, is the key to Africa's sustainable development.

In preparation for the 2009 UNESCO World Conference on Higher Education (WCHE), a task force established by ADEA and UNESCO identified several strategic orientations for African higher education. One of these was the creation of an African higher education and research area. The July 2009 Communiqué of WCHE, in its section on higher education in Africa, placed emphasis on the need to develop an African higher education and research area through innovative forms of collaboration, in addition to improving the quality of higher education and promoting academic mobility across the continent. Subsequently, the steering committee of ADEA's Working Group on Higher Education (WGHE), which Prof. Chilundo chairs, decided to explore the concept of creating an African higher education and research area through an analytical study in order to propose concrete actions for stakeholders.

The study to map the state of higher education in the five Portuguese speaking countries in Africa (PALOP) forms part of this analytical work. Its findings and recommendations will therefore contribute to a better understanding of what Africa needs to do to strengthen and sustain its higher education and research space. Furthermore, the findings are intended to serve as the basis for strengthening a sustainable higher education research and advocacy network amongst PALOP and between PALOP and other continental education and research networks. ADEA is pleased to share the results of this study in the hope that the strengthening of these and other sub-regional initiatives further the Association's mandate of a holistic approach to capacity building and education development in Africa.

Alice Sena Lamptey
WCHE, ADEA

Executive summary and structure

This report is the result of a baseline study on the state of art of the higher education (HE) systems in the five Portuguese speaking (Lusophone[1]) countries in Africa (PALOP): Angola, Cape Verde, Guinea-Bissau, Mozambique, and São Tomé and Príncipe. The project was undertaken by an African international expert in the field of higher education studies and was fully sponsored and supported by the Association for the Development of Education in Africa (ADEA).

The report offers a historical overview of the development of higher education in PALOP from colonial times to the present. The information and data contained in this report are based on the available higher education literature and official documents as well as interviews with key individuals in PALOP.

The main objective of the baseline study is to map the landscape and dynamics of change in the higher education systems of PALOP countries. It focuses on describing the latest developments in expansion trends, financing, governance and policy reforms closely linked to the development of higher education systems of these countries. Furthermore, the study brings knowledge that can facilitate and inform debate and the dissemination of knowledge on the role of higher education for development in Africa.

This baseline study is based on existing research and knowledge on dynamics of change in African higher education, and attempts to fill the existing knowledge gap with regard to Lusophone African countries. A process of stakeholder consultation and discussion constituted the hallmark of this project.

The report is organised into seven chapters, starting with an introduction, followed by five chapters focusing on each of the five PALOP countries, presented in alphabetical order, and finally a conclusion. Most importantly, Appendix 1 presents a short report advocating for the constitution of a platform for effective collaboration and network building among PALOP.

---

1   The Portuguese speaking countries in Africa are also known as *Lusophone* African countries.

CHAPTER 1

INTRODUCTION AND BACKGROUND

1.1 Introduction

This study was commissioned by ADEA and funded by the African Development Bank to fill the existing gap in information and data in the production of research in higher education in the Portuguese speaking countries in Africa (PALOP). The study was conceived in July 2011, with Prof. Arlindo Chilundo, the deputy minister of education for Mozambique and Ms Alice Sena Lamptey, coordinator of the Working Group at ADEA, playing a critical role in this regard.

PALOP have been neglected in current literature on higher education studies. There has been a dearth of comprehensive studies which fully address the developments and dynamics of change in PALOP. The few studies available on higher education in PALOP tend to integrate some of these countries in their particular geopolitical and economic location predominantly on an economic comparative basis. Accordingly, Angola and Mozambique would be integrated in the Southern African Community Development (SADC) region and therefore be compared to some of the other members, such as South Africa and Namibia. Cape Verde, Guinea-Bissau and São Tomé and Príncipe every so often would be regarded as small and insular states with their specificities integrated in their respective geopolitical and economic regions (Tolentino 2006).

This study examines some aspects of the historical development of higher education in these five countries and attempts to map the current dynamics of change in the field of higher education in these countries. It examines the process of establishing higher education institutions (HEIs), the regulatory framework and the governance structures of the system, and the information technology infrastructure in each of the five countries.

1.2   Objectives of the study

This study has three major objectives:
(i) to present an updated baseline study of the state of higher education in the five Portuguese speaking countries in Africa, focusing on the various elements that constitute a higher education system, viz., number of institutions, students, academics, regulatory framework, governance bodies etc.;
(ii) to analyse the current dynamics of change and the state of art of higher education in these countries; and
(iii) to create the basis for the establishment of a network for higher education research and advocacy in PALOP.

1.3   Methodology of the study

The methodological strategy for this study started with a desktop-based literature review to determine current trends in the development of higher education in PALOP. The objective is not to present a comparative analysis of the five countries, even if that were desirable and somehow achievable given the comparability of some of the data gathered. Rather, what we have in this document are five chapters each containing a case study mapping the development of higher education as a social institution in the five PALOP countries.

The methodology used to collect data is the following:
- Comprehensive desk research to gather the relevant documents about higher education in the five PALOP with emphasis on policy documents, research reports, academic papers, dissertations, conference proceedings, newspapers and magazines;
- Review of international literature on higher education;
- Site visits to capital cities of the five countries, namely Angola, Cape Verde, Guinea-Bissau, Mozambique, and São Tomé and Príncipe. I restricted the visits to the capital cities due to constraints of time and finances.
- During the site visits to the PALOP countries, I held meetings and interviews with key informants such as top government official related to (higher) education, and reputable academics in the field of (higher) education. Time constraints did not allow extending the list of interviewees.
- I conducted open and semi-structured interviews on some of the following topics:
    (i) The extent to which higher education reforms in the PALOP countries have led to expansion, institutional diversification and differentiation.
    (ii) The extent to which higher education reforms have had an impact on the structure and content of institutional programmes.
    (iii) The extent to which higher education reforms in PALOP are characterised by geographical and institutional decentralisation or fragmented expansion.
    (iv) What governance structures and steering mechanisms (policy, market, financing, international best practices) are guiding higher education reforms in PALOP?

(v) What are the levels of system coordination and integration with other sectors in the larger society?

(vi) The extent to which higher education reforms in PALOP are guided by policies that encourage diversification and differentiation and a linkage with national economies and labour markets.

(vii) The extent to which higher education expansion in PALOP serves the diverse skills needs of students as well as the needs of the national economies and labour markets.

(viii) What are the existing quality assurance strategies and mechanisms, and what are the perspectives on quality by policy makers, students, parents, employers and external stakeholders?

(ix) What levels of research and research cooperation and collaborations exist in PALOP, particularly in science, technology, innovation and information and communication technologies (ICTs)?

ANGOLA

2.1 Country profile

The Republic of Angola is a country situated in south-western Africa, bordered by Namibia to the south, Democratic Republic of Congo to the north, Zambia to the east and the Atlantic Ocean to the west. With a surface area of about 1 246 700 square km, Angola is the largest of the PALOP countries. In general, Angola's population data is not wholly reliable. The latest population census was conducted in 1970, during the colonial period. Data on population presented in this document is based on estimates by organisations such as *CIA World Factbook* and the United Nations and the Bertelsmann Transformation Index (BTI). The *CIA World Factbook* (2011) estimates that in 2011 Angola had a population of about 13 338 541; according to the United Nations (2008) the Angolan population was around 18 498 000 inhabitants; and for the BTI (2010) in 2009 the total population of the country was estimated at around 17 600 000 inhabitants.

Portuguese is the official language of the country, but the majority of Angolans speak Bantu languages, in particular Kikongo, Chokwe, Umbundu, Kimbundu, Ganguela and Kwanyama. Angola is divided into 18 provinces and 163 municipalities. Luanda is its capital city and also its main economic, political and cultural centre.

The country gained independence from Portuguese colonial rule on 11 November 1975 after nearly a decade of anti-colonial war waged by three nationalist movements, namely the MPLA (Popular Movement for the Liberation of Angola), UNITA (National Union for Total Independence of Angola) and the FNLA (National Front for the Liberation of Angola).

Immediately after independence a violent civil war broke out, pitting two of the country's anti-colonial movements against each other. These were the MPLA, the ruling party (supported by the Soviet Union and Cuba), and UNITA (supported mainly by apartheid South Africa and later the USA). The FNLA also participated in the conflict, but only during its early stages and to a lesser extent.

The civil war came to an end in 2002, after Jonas Malheiro Savimbi, UNITA's leader, was killed by MPLA government forces. The subsequent UNITA leadership, weakened by the death of their leader, negotiated peace with MPLA government officials and turned UNITA from a military movement into a political party.

In 2008 the country held its first multi-party elections, which were won by the MPLA and its candidate, José Eduardo dos Santos. Constitutionally, Angola is a presidential republic, and the president is head of both the government and the state. For the whole of its post-colonial history the country has been ruled by two presidents: Agostinho Neto ruled the country from independence unitl 1979, and the incumbent, José Eduardo dos Santos, has been in office since 1979 following the death of Neto.

Angola is one of the richest countries in Africa in terms of precious natural resources. It has extensive oil and gas resources, diamonds, hydroelectric potential and rich agricultural land. Despite these resources, the 27 years of civil war damaged the country's economic and social well-being. Since the end of the civil war, its socio-economic indicators have started to improve but, in general, the country remains poor. According to *The Economist*, from 2001 to 2010 Angola's GDP increased at an annual rate of 11%, making it one of the fastest growing economies in the world (*The Economist* 2011).

The oil sector contributes over 50% of economic growth. In 2010, Angola's nominal GDP was around USD 85.81 million and its per capita nominal GDP was around USD 4 477 (IMF 2010). Concerning social indicators, the *CIA World Factbook* (2011) provides the following data: life expectancy: 38.78 years; child mortality rate: 180/1 000. For the United Nations Development Programme Report (UNDP 2010), in 2010, Angola's Human Development Index (HDI) was low at 0.403, putting the country in 149th position in a list of 192 countries. The UNDP report for 2009 (UNDP 2009) estimates that the country's literacy rate was about 67.4% in 2009. This data is somehow different from the one presented by the BTI (2010), concerning 2009: life expectancy: 47 years; HDI: 0.560 (rank 143); percentage of people living with less than USD 2 a day: 70.2%; GDP per capita: USD 5 163.

2.2 Background and historical context of higher education

The history of higher education (HE) in Angola dates back to the colonial period. In 1962, the Portuguese colonial authorities established the first HEI, Estudos Gerais Universitários de Angola (EGUA), by Decree Law 44 530, as part of the Portuguese system of higher education, offering courses in agriculture, forestry, civil engineering, medicine, veterinary medicine and education. In 1968, the EGUA was renamed Universidade de Luanda (UNL) and after the proclamation of independence and the creation of a new government, in 1975, UNL became the Universidade de Angola (UNA) in 1976. Later, in 1985, the university was again renamed and became the Universidade Agostinho Neto (UAN) in honour of the first president of the country, Dr Antonio Agostinho Neto (De Carvalho, Kajibanga and Heimer 2003). UAN remained the only public higher education institution (HEI) in the country until 1999 when private universities were established. By then it had established campuses in 7 of Angola's 18 provinces: Luanda, Huambo, Huíla, Benguela, Uíge, Cabinda and Kwanza Sul.

2.3 Trends of expansion, diversification and differentiation

Expansion, diversification and differentiation are among the recurrent concepts utilised to account for the dynamics of change in higher education systems (Schofer and Meyer 2005). The notion of expansion in higher education basically refers to the rapid growth in the number of students that create pressures for a shift to a mass, open, post-secondary education system (Scott 1995). Diversity and differentiation are the flip side of the same coin and a consequence of expansion. According to Van Vught (2007), differentiation as a concept should be distinguished from the concept of diversity. For Van Vught, diversity is a term indicating the variety of entities within a system; while differentiation denotes a dynamic process, diversity refers to a static situation. Thus, as pointed out by Huisman (1995: 51, quoted in Van Vught 2007: 2), while differentiation refers to the process by which new entities in a system emerge, diversity refers to the variety of the entities at a specific point in time.

As of 1999, and particularly from 2002 onwards, following peace agreements, the private sector began to participate actively in the expansion and diversification of the Angolan higher education system. In 1999, three new higher education institutions (HEIs) were established – Universidade Católica de Angola (UCA), Universidade Lusíada de Angola (ULA), Universidade Jean Piaget de Angola (UJP) – and from 2002 until 2009, 13 more private HEIs were established – Universidade de Belas (UNB), Universidade Técnica de Angola (UTA), Instituto Superior Técnico de Angola (ISTA), Universidade Metodista de Angola (UNMA), Universidade Independente de Angola (UNIA), Universidade Privada de Angola (UNPA), Universidade Gregório Semedo (UGS), Universidade Óscar Ribas (UOR), Instituto Superior de Ciências Sociais e Relações Internacionais (ISCSRI), Instituto Superior Dom Bosco (ISDB), Instituto Superior Técnico (IST), Instituto Superior João Paulo II (ISJP II) and Universidade Metropolitana (UNM).

In 2009, the government undertook actions designed to expand and diversify the public higher education sector: the only public HEI, Universidade Agostinho Neto, was restructured and gave birth to seven autonomous public HEIs, settled in seven academic regions (RAS 2009)[1] – Universidade Agostinho Neto, settled in Luanda and Bengo; Universidade Katyavala Buila, in Benguela and Kwanza Sul; Universidade de 11 Novembro, in Cabinda and Zaire; Universidade Lueji A'Nkonden, in Lunda Norte, Lunda Sul and Malanje; Universidade José Eduado dos Santos, in Huambo, Bié and Moxico; Universidade Madume Ya Ndemofayo, in Huila, Namibe, Cunene, Kuando; and Universidade Kimpa Vita, in Uige and Kwanza Norte (Nascimento 2012, interview; RAS 2009).

By the end of 2010, there were at least 23 HEIs in Angola, seven of which were public and 16 private. However, the total number of HEIs may be higher than 23: year after year, new

---

1 A recent education reform has divided Angola into seven different academic regions, the goal being to have at least one HE facility in each of them by 2012. The reform created new institutions, while at the same time restructuring Luanda's Agostinho Neto University (UAN) (interview with Dias Nascimento, 22 February 2012).

institutions, in particular private ones, are established, as the following citation, from the online newspaper *O País*, illustrates:

> *Despite the legal requirements and conditions demanded, the number of universities and higher institutes continues to increase at a frightening speed. In addition to the new universities opening their gates this academic year, there are others waiting for answers from the authorities to join the existing ones.* (Costa 2009a, b)

This citation suggests that the increase of HEIs in Angola is still taking place.

Notwithstanding the requirements or conditions required by law, the number of universities and colleges continues to grow in a way that concerns some government officials and academics. While arguing that the Angolan system of higher education has experienced an impressive growth, De Carvalho (2009) and Nascimento (22 February 2012, interview) also acknowledge that this development was not followed by the appropriate measures to ensure the quality of the courses and programmes offered by these institutions. Both scholars think that the state should play a more visible and significant role in regulating the system and not leave it up to market forces. On the other hand, despite the growth in the number of institutions, the system still excludes a large number of prospective students. UAN is by far Angola's biggest university, with more than 60 000 students at its main campus and its 17 branches spread around the country. In 2002 the university had a total of 9 000 students.

The number of places available at the branches increased to 8 900 in 2009, from 7 000 in 2008. The rise in places available at the branches and at the main campus is still not enough to meet demand. In Luanda in 2009, there were 11 applicants for each available space. To make room for more students, a new 5 000-acre campus, which will accommodate 40 000 students, is being built on the outskirts of the city (*O País* 2012). The new campus has a library measuring 8 500 square metres, in addition to conference halls, research centres for advanced studies, and infrastructure, maintenance and operation areas. In terms of academics, the campus houses nine faculties, including arts, architecture, economics, law, medicine and oil. Chemistry, physics, mathematics and computer studies will be the first courses offered at the facility which covers 360 000 square metres.

2.3.1 Institutions and programmes

In this section, I summarise the historical development of the higher education system in Angola from 1975 to 2010. The key markers of the historical development of the country's higher education in this period are summarised below. In 1962 the first HEI was established: the *Estudos Gerais Universitários de Angola* (EGUA). In 1963 the head offices of the EGUA were still the colonial metropolis, Portugal. There were no management structures on Angolan territory. The courses and programmes offered included: agriculture, forestry and veterinary medicine in Huambo Province (former Nova Lisboa); arts, geography, pedagogy and Roman studies in Huila Province (former Sá da Bandeira); science, medical surgery, and preparatory courses in industrial, chemistry, civil, electrical and mining engineering) in

Luanda (former of district of Luanda). In 1965 for the first time a Rector's office was established in Luanda. Three years later, the EGUA gained full university status as the University of Luanda. In 1969, the university hospital and national library were inaugurated in Luanda. In 1970 the university opened the Faculty of Economics. In 1975 during the transition to independence teaching at the university was temporarily interrupted.

2.3.2 The establishment of Agostinho Neto University (ANU)

The Universidade Agostinho Neto is the *alma mater* public Angolan university based in the capital, Luanda. Until 2009 it had campuses in all major Angolan cities. In 2009 the university's campuses outside Luanda were transformed into autonomous universities. These were in Benguela, Cabinda, Huambo, Lubango, Malange and Uíge. Today, the university has campuses only in Luanda and Bengo Provinces, and remains the largest university in Angola. While until 2000 its only competitor was the Catholic University of Angola, it currently faces competition from about a dozen private universities. In the academic year 2005/2006, 68 approved courses were offered by the university. Eighteen of these courses were offered at Bachelors degree level and 15 at Masters degree level, and the remaining were *Licenciaturas* (Bachelor Honours).

Table 2.1 Public universities in Angola 2012

Public institution	Location
Agostinho Neto University (UNA)	Luanda and Bengo
Katyavala Buíla University	Benguela and Kuanza Sul
11 November University	Zaire and Cabinda
Lueji A'Nkonda University	Lunda Norte, Lunda Sul and Malange
Kimpa Vita University	Úige e Kuanza-Norte
José Eduardo dos Santos University	Huambo, Bié and Mexico
Mandume Ya Ndemofayo University	Huíla, Cunene, Kuando-Kubango and Namibe

Source: RAS 2009

2.3.3 The emergence of private universities

Private universities emerged in Angola in the 1990s, but their number multiplied after 2007. There are now more than 20 private institutions in the country. By January 2012 Angola's ministry of higher education, science and technology recognised the private HEIs in the table overleaf.

The council of ministers rules on the establishment of private universities. However, comments from the ministry of education, science and technology and the secretary of state for higher education seem to indicate that not all regulations and guidelines that govern the

Table 2.2 Private higher education institutions in Angola 2011

	Private institution	Decree and year of establishment
1	Gregório Semedo University (Samba)	Decreto no 22/2007; Dr 1a Série no 55 de 07 de Maio
2	Óscar Ribas University (Samba)	Decreto no 27/2007; Dr 1a Série no 55 de 07 de Maio
3	Belas University of Angola (UNIBELAS) (Samba)	Decreto no 25/2007; Dr 1a Série no 55 de 07 de Maio
4	Independent University of Angola (Samba)	Decreto no 11/2005; Dr 1a Série no 43 de 11 de Abril
5	Institute for Science and International Relations (CIS)(Samba)	Decreto no 26/2007; Dr 1a Série no 55 de 07 de Maio
6	Metropolitan University (Samba)	Decreto no 110/11; Dr 1a Série no 149 de 5 de Agosto
7	Institute John Paul II (Maianga)	–
8	Higher Technical Institute (ISTEA)	Decreto no 113/2011; Dr 1a Série no 149 de 5 de Agosto
9	Methodist University (UMA)(Ingombota)	Decreto no 30/2007; Dr 1a Série no 55 de 07 de Maio
10	Lusíada University (ULA)(Ingombota)	Decreto no 42-A/2002; Dr 1a Série no 66 de 20 de Agosto
11	Private University of Angola (UPRA) (Cazenga)	Decreto no 28/2007; Dr 1a Série no 55 de 07 de Maio
12	Instituto Superior Técnico (ISTEA) (Cazenga campus)	Decreto no 24/2007; Dr 1a Série no 55 de 07 de Maio
13	Technical University of Angola (UTANGA) (Kilamba Kiaxi)	Decreto no 29/2007; Dr 1a Série no 55 de 07 de Maio
14	Catholic University of Angola (UCAN) (Palanca)	Decreto no 38-A/1992; Dr Suplemento de 07 de Agosto
15	Jean Piaget University (Viana)	Decreto no 44-A/2001; 1a Série no 30 de 6 de Junho
16	Don Bosco Institute (Sambizanga)	
17	Polytechnic Institute of Benguela	Decreto no 109/2011; Dr 1a Série no 149 de 5 de Agosto
18	Polytechnic Institute of Technology and Science	Decreto no 111/2011; Dr 1a Série no 149 de 5 de Agosto
19	Polytechnic Institute of Humanities and Technology – II Ekuikui	Decreto no 112/2011; Dr 1a Série no 149 de 5 de Agosto
20	Polytechnic Tundavala Higher Institute	Decreto no 114/2011; Dr 1a Série no 149 de 5 de Agosto
21	Polytechnic Institute of Kangojo	Decreto no 115/2011; Dr 1a Série no 149 de 5 de Agosto
22	Polytechnic Independent Higher Institute	Decreto no 116/2011; Dr 1a Série no 149 de 5 de Agosto
23	Polytechnic Pangea Higher Institute	Decreto no 1117/2011; Dr 1a Série no 149 de 5 de Agosto
24	Polytechnic Institute of Gregory Semedo	Decreto no 118/2011; Dr 1a Série no 149 de 5 de Agosto

Source: MESCT 2012

opening of private universities in Angola have been adhered to (Nascimento 22 February 2012, interview). According to Nascimento (2012) this has resulted in inadequate facilities, lack of resources and study materials, libraries, laboratories and appropriate courses, and overall a sub-standard level of quality in the tertiary education sector. There are also too few staff to service the number of universities, with the result that many teach (illegally) at more than one university (Costa 2009a). According to *O País*, in June 2010 tuition fees for private universities in Luanda ranged between USD 2 750 and USD 3 850 per year (minimum), excluding the registration fee. This compares unfavourably with regional competitors such as Namibia (USD 1 500–2 000 per year) and South Africa (USD 2 000 per year), where study materials such as textbooks and other materials are also generally included in the fee (Costa 2009b).

2.4 Changes in higher education governance

This section examines particular changes to the structures of higher education governance in Angola. It focuses especially on policies, regulations and responsibilities in the governance of HEIs in the country. The analysis is limited to a broad description of major changes in governance and management structures. It describes the key features of higher education governance in Angola, the various types of governance structures in the country, and the strengths and weaknesses of these governance structures.

2.4.1 Changing governance contexts

2.4.1.1 Late colonialism: Higher education for settlers

Unlike other colonial powers who foresaw African independence and either sluggishly prepared for it or tried to delay it for as long as possible, Portugal nursed the dream of ruling Africa forever. This experiment was tested in Angola and Mozambique. The 1951 constitution officially made Portugal an 'Afro-European' power. As a result, Angola and Mozambique became Portuguese provinces, very much like De Gaulle's 'France d'outremer' or overseas France (Fowale 2009). In 1962, soon after the start of the African wars of independence, the Portuguese government founded the first institution of higher education in Angola and Mozambique. The General University Studies of Angola and Mozambique catered to the sons and daughters of Portuguese colonists. Although the Portuguese government preached non-racism and advocated the assimilation of its African subjects to the Portuguese way of life, to give a more human face to its prolonged colonial rule, the notorious deficiencies of the colonial education system established under Portuguese rule ensured that very few Africans would ever succeed in reaching university level (Mário et al. 2003, Beverjik 2005, Langa 2006). Portugal kept enrolments very low, and places were primarily offered to the sons and daughters of Portuguese colonialists.

2.4.1.2 Independence and the socialist experiment: Central planning and the birth of the developmental university

Higher education in Angola really only began in any meaningful sense with independence. Portuguese colonial education was conceived as a system that produced an ideological dependence and subjection, and changed Angola into an exporter territory of raw material and cheap labour to Europe's industrial countries and its allies (Neto 2005). This is similar to most African colonies which had no universities as they approached independence (Mamdani 2008, Langa 2006, Beverjik 2005). As the number of HEIs in Angola expanded, the governance and management structures had to be adjusted to the new reality. Until recently, the governance of Angolan higher education was reduced to the governance of Angostinho Neto University. With the expansion of UAN beyond Luanda, Huambo and Huila, where it had established branches, new governance structures at provincial level were put in place (MED 2005). By the 1990s governance and management of higher education in Angola was limited to the authority and administration of the Agostinho Neto University (UAN), since UAN was the sole HEI in the country (MED 2005).

2.4.1.3 From war to neoliberal reform

For more than three decades Angola was devastated by a protracted civil war. Until 1990 the war which started before independence was conditioned by the international conflict between the East and West (the Cold War), and simultaneously by the regional policy of South Africa's apartheid regime. After a series of agreements among the parties involved in the conflict, elections held in 1992 led to the establishment of a multiparty democracy, and the end of what was then termed the 'First Republic' (De Carvalho et al. 2003).

Like in many other countries, the attempt to create a socialist society in Angola failed. During the first decade of independence the economic regime was one of state or collective property and centralised planning and control. The combination of civil war and economic difficulties soon led to an almost total stagnation of the country, with severe effects. As a result, education declined steadily. In the late 1980s and early 1990s the country began a process of liberalising the economy. The liberalisation of the higher education sector followed, and many laws and regulations were enacted.

In 1990, decree 90/09 of 15 December established the norms and regulations for Angolan higher education. This decree repealed decrees 35/01 and 65/04 of 8 June 1935 and 22 October 1965, respectively. These were colonial and socialist legislations that contradicted the spirit of liberalisation of decree 90/09 (Decree 90/90). The national legal and regulative framework was changed to accommodate radical changes in Angolan higher education.

According to De Carvalho et al. (2003), one of the main challenges facing higher education in Angola since independence has been political interference. The ruling party has been involved in the 'hiring and firing' of teaching staff. Only party members of strong Marxist-Leninist convictions were appointed to teach in the social and human sciences. The authors argued that the university was strongly influenced by Angola's politics. This impression depicts the Angolan higher education as one of limited academic freedom and institutional autonomy.

In 1992, the only existing university had the status of a public entity dependent on the ministry of education. Its dependency was political as well as administrative. Its rector and vice-rectors were appointed by the president of the republic, upon the proposal of the ruling party, the MPLA; the rector had the political status of a vice-minister. The directors of the different schools were appointed by the minister of education, also at the suggestion of the MPLA. The university was supposed to apply the policies and guidelines of the MPLA, that is, to plan and implement the government activities in the field of higher education, and to guarantee teaching, research and diffusion of scientific knowledge (De Carvalho et al. 2003). However, De Carvalho et al. (2003) argue that the political changes introduced from the early 1990s onwards led to changes in the governing of higher education, with institutions experiencing more autonomy. In 1995 legislation conferring full autonomy to universities was passed. Thus universities ceased to be institutionally subjected to orders from the MPLA or the ministry of education. De Carvalho *et al.* (2003) suggest that a system of internal democracy was introduced in institutions, allowing free election of collegial boards and office holders by the teaching staff. It also allowed for the selection of teaching staff based exclusively on academic merit. The influence of politics in academia has somewhat improved following the political developments of the mid-1990s, when the Angolan government conferred to the university, in 1995, a new legal status and organic structure. Its nature and mission were redefined as being those of an 'entity of public law, having statutory, scientific, pedagogical, administrative, financial and disciplinary autonomy, designed for the formation of high level cadres in the different fields of knowledge' (Decree 90/1990).

The period from 2002 to 2010 was mainly marked by the following legal and political changes in Angolan higher education which altered the governance structures and mechanisms:

- 2003: Establishment of the national directorate of higher education in the structure of the ministry of education
- 2005: Appointment of a deputy minister of education in higher education
- 2006: Guidelines for the reform and improvement of higher education
- 2007: Establishment of the state secretariat for higher education
- 2009: Resizing of Agostinho Neto University and the establishment of new public HEIs by academic regions
- 2010: Establishment of the ministry of higher education and science and technology

These are the main changes in the governance structure in place in Angolan higher education.

2.4.2   Quality assurance

Quality assurance in Angolan higher education has been an issue of concern since the mid-1980s. In the pathway of the development of higher education in Angola there are references that indicate the existence of concerns related to quality, particularly following the liberalisation of the subsector. In 1986, and again ten years later in 1996, two foundations commissioned studies by Gomes Teixeira (1996) and Calouste Gulbenkian Foundation (1986) to assess the state of quality in the country's higher education system. In 2005 another assessment was carried out by the secretary of state for higher education (SEES).

The outcome of the assessment by SEES formed the basis for the development of guidelines for improving the management of HEIs in Angola. It also served as the rationale for the restructuring of UAN, resulting in six separate public universities. Institutional assess-ment has been raised as an instrument which would give the possibility of greater state regulation of the subsystem, and as a means of improving quality. Considerable legislation was passed to regulate the system as well as to assure that minimum quality standards are met.

The issue of quality assurance gained more relevance and specificity with the establishment of the National Board for Higher Education, whose responsibility includes, among others, to 'ensure the quality and efficiency of the subsystem' (Article 18, Decree-Law 7/03, 17 June). Despite these developments, Angola still does not have an integrated quality assurance system that oversees the entire subsystem of higher education. There is, however, growing concern and awareness from the government about the need to develop a quality assurance system.

A more structured framework for institutional assessment was designed and is regulated by Decree-Law 2/2009, 29 April. This framework is under the organisational structure of the SEES as the technical entity responsible for assessment and quality control, evaluation and accreditation. This unit is charged with monitoring and promoting the quality of services provided by HEIs, and with coordinating institutional evaluations and accreditation (Decree-Law 2/09, 29 April). This unit was the first organisational structure established to oversee quality in Angolan higher education. Recent developments, particularly the approval of the new constitution in 2010, saw this unit being relocated under the newly established ministry of higher education, science and technology (MESCT). The Institute for Quality Assurance and Accreditation of Higher Education was then established under the tutelage of MESCT (Art. 24, Presidential Decree 70/10, 19 May).

The governance of Angolan higher education is characterised by uneven changes in terms of the structures and institutions mandates, from MESCT to SEES, therefore delaying the implementation of policies. The implementation of the quality assurance mechanisms prescribed by some of the legislation continues to be delayed. Since the establishment of the Institute for Quality Assurance and Accreditation in 2010 no real activity towards quality assessment has taken place.

2.5 Financing higher education

After about 30 years of neglect during the civil war, education has seen heavy public investment. The government has also expanded vocational/technical education to address massive skill shortages. Furthermore, tertiary education has experienced exponential growth, with enrolment in higher education growing by more than 50% per year since 2002, to 140 000 in 2011.

A range of practices for determining higher education budget allocations for recurrent and investment expenditures can be found around the world. In addition to historically-based budgeting, they include earmarked funding, input-based formulas, performance-based formulas, performance contracts and competitive funds. Although some African countries have experimented with these other approaches, these are the exception rather than the rule.Most African nations have yet to attempt any innovation in their budget allocation methods (World Bank 2010).

According to the World Bank (2010) the most common approach to operational budgeting for universities is to use the previous year or years as a baseline and make incremental changes based on general considerations such as the country's economic performance, government revenues, inflation rates or institutional growth. This approach was widespread in Africa during the 1990s and continues today in many African countries including Angola, Ethiopia, Lesotho, Madagascar, Mauritania and Mozambique.

In Africa, two distinct types of dual-track tuition fee policies are being implemented. The first type, used by countries such as Ghana, Uganda, Tanzania and Kenya, awards free or low-cost places to a limited number of students based on their performance on the secondary school-leaving exam, and fee-paying places to others who score lower but still meet entrance criteria or, as in Angola and Ethiopia, to those who study in the evening or during the summer. The second type, used by countries such as Benin, Madagascar and Senegal, offers free places to all students passing the high school-leaving baccalaureate exam in faculties with open access, and fee-paying places in the more competitive professional faculties or institutions. As referred above, Angola used the first type of fee policy, that is, the dual-track fee. The regular students pay no fees, and evening (part-time) students pay market-related fees, as do those studying at private HEIs.

2.5.1 Sources of funding and expenditure on higher education

Angola's HEIs have four main sources of funding. These are: state appropriations; student fees; contributions from private and international donors; and paid services to individual or corporate users (De Carvalho *et al.* 2003). The higher education public sector is predominantly financed by the state. Private HEIs depend mainly on tuition fees and other fees paid by students. A UNDP 2002 report, entitled 'Public financing in social sectors in Angola', indicates that the ministry of finance, except in a few cases, deals directly with the budget units of the sector, which are mainly the *institutos médios*[2], the faculties and other HEIs, the autonomous national institutes (such as the Instituto Nacional de Bolsas de Estudos[3]) and the central structure of the ministry of education and culture (UNDP 2002).

Table 2.6 below shows the expenditure on higher education between 2004 and 2008 in Angolan Kwanzas (USD 1 = AOA 96.00).

Table 2.3 Expenditure on higher education 2004 to 2008 (AOA)

Amount	2004 %	2005 %	2006 %	2007 %	2008 %
Budget	69 637 027 100%	55 561 821 100%	85 523 557 100%	140 394 653 100%	200 620 366 100%
Higher Education	4 524 661 6.5%	7 413 593 13.3%	7 768 011 9.1%	12 914 856 9.2%	18 390 613 9.2%

Source: MINFIN 2012

The one indicator provided is not sufficient to make consistent claims about the significance of the increase in the budget allocated to higher education. However, there is a clear indication of an increase in the percentage of funds allocated to higher education on annual basis.

An analysis of the intra-sectoral distribution of funding shows a distorting effect caused by the amount allocated to scholarships. A major distorting factor in the distribution of

---

2   Colleges or training institutes.
3   http://www.inabe.gov.ao/

resources within the education system is the importance given to scholarships. For instance, Table 2.4 shows that, between 1997 and 2001, scholarships took up 18% of the resources provided to the sector, which was equivalent to half of the value of expenditure on basic education (UNDP 2002). According to the UNDP (2002) report, from 1997 to 2000 the amounts provided for scholarships to study abroad exceeded the funding provided for higher education within the country (see Table 2.4). The high percentage of expenditure on scholarships, which has no parallel in other African countries, is quite simply out of proportion, especially when account is taken of the huge resources that would have to be mobilised to achieve the goal of universal primary school enrolment as well as the needs of other levels of the education system within the country. Although the country needs a balanced education system, with adequate capacity beyond the primary level, it would be more efficient and equitable to train a larger number of students at tertiary level within the country, by developing the university faculties and institutes, than to send a relatively small number of students abroad at enormous cost and with a high risk of non-return on the part of the beneficiaries.

Table 2.4 Education expenditure across subsectors 1997–2001 (USD)

Programmes	1997	1998	1999	2000	2001
General administration	102 109	89 416	68 137	133 276	182 051
Educational assistance	19 245	–	–	–	–
Basic education (*ensino de base*)	10 416	2 308	2 624	7 164	–
Special education	–	4 409	1 767	4 190	5 786
Intermediate education (*ensino medio*)	–	3 793	3 094	12 651	–
Supplemental education	1 380	612	362	1 223	–
Professional training	–	695	851	2 386	–
Higher education	12 535	12 621	13 401	22 856	19 378
School network	4 660	–	–	–	–
Scholarships	–	13 192	46 141	30 285	44 913
Public investment	–	–	–	–	15 129
Others	4 948	6 738	6 820	8 799	34 623
Total	155 294	133 786	143 198	222 829	301 880

Source: UNDP 2002

2.5.2   Tuition fees and cost-sharing

The type of tuition fee policy adopted by a country has implications for the kinds of financial aid policies that are put in place to ensure access for its most vulnerable groups. Typically, an 'up-front tuition policy' (and/or registration fees) requires students (or parents or extended families) to pay a tuition fee for a semester or academic year at the beginning of that semester or year (World Bank 2010). Higher education reforms adopted in most African countries indicate cost-reduction measures, cost-sharing strategies and income-generating strategies (Varghese 2001, Wangenge-Ouma and Cloete 2008).

In most African countries a cost-sharing strategy is progressively being incorporated in funding strategies of the tertiary education sector (Wangenge-Ouma 2007, Pillay 2010). As of 2009 at least 26 countries in Africa charge either up-front tuition fees or other types of fees, such as examination fees, registration fees, identity-card fees, library fees and management information system fees. When up-front tuition fees are particularly difficult to implement, some governments prefer dual track tuition policies, whereby a certain number of free (or very low cost) university places are awarded, based on some criteria such as academic excellence, income level or positive discrimination, and other places are available on a tuition fee-paying basis, or deferred tuition policy. In Angola, government adopted the dual track tuition fee policy where no tuition fees are charged to the regular students, but tuition fees are charged in the evening study programmes (World Bank 2010). The average monthly tuition paid in private HEIs was about USD 250.

2.6   Access and equity

Since the colonial era, access to higher education has been for the privileged in Angola. After independence, the demand for access to the only HEI, the Agostinho Neto University, was far higher than the institution's capacity to accommodate students. Access was basically free of charge during the first years of independence, since Government was pursuing a socialist model of centralised economy. The entry requirements for higher education changed over time. In 1992 the Rector of UAN was given the authority to establish the admission criteria. According to De Carvalho *et al.* (2003: 168) 'a *numerus clausus* was established for all study programmes and specific admission exams were defined for each programme'. Each school would have the authority to define core subjects and the content of the admission exams. Since 1999, *numerus clauses* have become a prerogative of each school to define. Minimal scores of 14 marks out of 20. (70%) were set as the entry criteria to higher education. This trend in access changed with the increasing number of private providers. Private providers of education would charge market fees to their clientele. The tuition fees and admission criteria would then depend on the financial ability of the students and their families. The primary condition to accessing private higher education is the ability to pay monthly fees. Private universities would charge a monthly fee ranging from USD 200 to USD 350.

Despite the liberalisation of the higher education sector to allow private providers, as one of the strategies for strengthening and creating more higher education space to expand access, the participation rate in higher education for Angola remains low (SARUA 2008).

In 2005, the gross enrolment ratios in higher education in Angola was 1% compared to 3% for Kenya, Uganda and Burundi; Mozambique and Tanzania 1%; Botswana 6% (Ishengoma 2011). Needless to say, very few Angolans have the ability to finance their studies, making access to higher learning a reserve of the privileged in society.

2.7 ICT in Angolan higher education

The ICT infrastructure in Angola can be described as developing, but with major challenges to overcome. According to Isaacs (2007):

> *Three decades of civil war have decimated the country's infrastructure and education system with large sections of the population still in dire straits, and high numbers of school-age children are out of school. Amid these challenges, the government has established a National Commission on Information Technology, now called the National IT Agency, which has been given the task of developing a national ICT policy. There are a few programmes and projects specifically on ICTs in education in the country, although these are largely small-scale, short-term initiatives.*

Angola is celebrating ten years of peace after the ceasefire that ended a violent three-decade conflict. In these ten years (2002 to 2012) several initiatives have been developed and many are still on-going to improve the quality of education in Angola, including the recognition of ICT as an important element of capacity development for Angolan society. Angola developed a national ICT policy, but little reference is made specifically to higher education.

Angola's ICT sector is developing rapidly, although general public access to services is still a challenge. There are several telecommunications operators (with state-owned Angola Telecom as the main service provider) and a national sector regulator, Inacom. Internet provision is open and relatively competitive, despite international traffic bottlenecks derived from limited connecting capacity to the international backbone. A major submarine cable following Angola's coastline is set to boost the coastal cities' access to internet and communications. A network of subsidised public phones is made available by the private fixed-line operators to increase access to ICT for poorer communities (ORSB 2011).

2.7.1 ICT policy development in Angola

Table 2.5 Progress made towards ICT implementation in recent years

Year	Event
1999	Establishment of the National Regulator Authority – INACOM (Decree No 12/99, 25 June 1999)
2000	Approval of the National Strategic Plan for the Development of ICT
2002	Establishment of the National Commission for Information Technology (D.R Iª Serie, No 24, 4 April 2002)
2006	Approval of the Information Society Action Plan and e-Gov Action Plan (D.R. Iª série, No 101, 21 August 2006)
2008	Establishment of the Ministry of Telecommunications and Information Technologies
2009	National Centre of IT, CNTI
2010	Approval of the New Statute for the MESCT by a Presidential Decree No 70/10, May 19 – Gazette. Series I – No. 93 – Approves the Organic Statute of MESCT

With the establishment of MESCT a new era begins in Angolan higher education governance. Government officials emphasised the need to establish quality assurance mechanisms in the country. Establishing and implementing quality assurance mechanisms seems to be main objective of the current higher education leadership in Angola (Texeira 2012).

REFERENCES

BIT (2010) Angola Country Report. Available at: http://www.bertelsmann-transformation-index.de/fileadmin/pdf/Gutachten_BTI2010/ESA/Angola.pdf [accessed 23 August 2010].

CIA WorldFact book (2011) *The CIA World Factbook on Angola*. Available at: https://www.cia.gov/library/publications/the-world-factbook/geos/ao.html [accessed 22 August 2011].

Costa D (2009a) Universidades para o Inglês ver. *O Pais*. Available at: http://www.opais.net/pt/dossier/?det=12099&id=2025 [accessed April 2012].

Costa D (2009b) Universidades para o Inglês ver. *O Pais*. Available at: http://www.opais.net/pt/opais/?id=1657&det=2843 [accessed: April 2012].

De Carvalho P, Kajibanga V and Heimer F (2003) Angola. In: Teferra D and Altbach P (eds) *African Higher Education. An International Reference Handbook*. Bloomington and Indianapolis: Indiana University Press, pp. 162–175.

Fowale T J (2009) Portuguese Colonialism in Africa: An unsuccessful experiment in everlasting rule. Available at: http://tongkeh-joseph-fowale.suite101.com/portuguese-colonialism-in-africa-a114429#ixzz1sGjMppPT [accessed April 2012].

Fundação Gomes Texeira (1996) *Contributos para a Revitalização da Universidade em Angola*. Porto: Publicações da Universidade do Porto.

Fundação Calouste Gulbenkian (1987) *Universidade Agostinho Neto: Estudo Global*. Lisboa: Fundação Calouste Gulbenkian.

Instituto Nacional de Estatística de Angola (INE-AO) (2012) Available at: http://www.ine-ao.com/censo.html [accessed April 2012].

International Monetary Fund (2011) Available at: http://www.imf.org [accessed 23 August 2011].

Isaacs S (2007) ICT in Education in Angola. *Survey of ICT and Education in Africa: Angola country report*. Available at: https://www.cia.gov/cia/publications/factbook/geos/ao.html [accessed April 2012].

Ishengoma J (2011) *Strengthening Higher Education Space in Africa through North–South Partnerships and Links: Myths and realities from Tanzanian public universities*. Available at: http://events.aau.org/userfiles/file/corevip11/papers/johnson_ishegoma_Creating_AHES.pdf [accessed April 2012].

King R (2009) *Governing Universities Globally: Organisations, regulation and rankings*. Cheltenham: Edward Elgar.

Langa P (2006) The Constitution of the Field of Higher Education Institutions in Mozambique. Masters dissertation. Cape Town: University of Cape Town.

Mamdani M (2008) Higher Education, the State and the Marketplace. *JHEA/RESA*, 6(1): 1–10.

Ministério da Educação (MED) (2005) *LINHAS MESTRAS para a melhoria da gestão do subsistema do Ensino Superior*. Luanda: Secretaria de Estado Para o Ensino Superior.

Neto MB (2005) História e educação em Angola: da ocupação colonial ao MPLA. Unpublished PhD thesis. Campinas: Universidade Estadual de Campinas.

O País (5 January 2012) *Campus da Camama com portas abertas*. Available at: http://ensinoangola.com/category/ensino-superior/ [accessed April 2012].

ORSB (2001) Angola country strategy paper 2011–2015. Available at: http://www.afdb.org/fileadmin/uploads/afdb/Documents/Project-and Operations/ORSB%20Angola%20CSP%202011%20 %202015%20En%20Rev%20Version%2BMemox.pdf [accessed April 2012].

Pillay P (ed.) (2010) *Higher Education Financing in East and Southern Africa*. Cape Town: African Minds.

RAS (2009) Novas universidades públicas de Angola e respectivos Colégios Reitorais Vide 'Reforma do ensino superior em Angola' Revista Angolana de Sociologia, 3: 185–188.

Schofer E and Meyer JW (2005) *World-Wide expansion of higher education*. Available at: http://iis-db.stanford.edu/pubs/20801/Schofer-Meyer_No32.pdf [accessed 30 April 2012].

Scott P (1995) *The Meanings of Mass Higher Education*. London: Open University Press.

Texeira PCM (2012) Discurso de Abertura de sua Excelência, Ministra do Ensino Superior e da Ciência e Tecnologia *Seminário Metodológico sobre Avaliação e Acreditação do Ensino Superior*. Available at: http://www.mesct.gov.ao/VerPublicacao.aspx?id=854 [accessed March 2012].

The Economist (2011) Africa's Impressive Growth. Available at: http://www.economist.com/blogs/dailychart/2011/01/daily_chart [accessed 30 April 2011].

UN (2008) Retrieved from the United Nations' Department of Economic and Social Affairs Population Division (2008), World Population Prospects, Table A. Available at: http://www.un.org/esa/population/publications/wpp2008/wpp2008_text_tables.pdf [accessed 22 August 2011].

UNDP (2002) *Public Financing of the Social Sectors in Angola*. Available at: http://mirror.undp.org/angola/LinkRtf/Public%20financing%20of%20the%20social%20sectors%20in%20Angola.pdf [accessed April 2012].

UNDP (2011) *Human Development Index 2010*. Available at: http://hdr.undp.org/en/media/Lets-Talk-HD-HDI_2010.pdf [accessed 23 August 2011].

UNDP (2009) *Human Development Report*. Available at: http://hdr.undp.org/en/media/HDR_2009_EN_Complete.pdf (Table H) [accessed 23 August 2011].

Van Vught F (2007) Diversity and Differentiation in Higher Education Systems. Available at: http://www.universityworldnews.com/filemgmt_data/files/Frans-van-Vucht.pdf [accessed 30 April 2012].

Varghase NV (2001) *Limits of Diversification of Sources of Funding in Higher Education*. IIEP contributions 34. Paris: IIEP.

Wangenge-Ouma G (2007) Reducing Resource Dependence on Government Funding: The case of Public Universities in Kenya and South Africa. Unpublished doctoral dissertation. University of Cape Town.

Wangenge-Ouma G and Cloete N (2008) Financing Higher Education in South Africa: Public funding, non-government revenue and tuition fees. *South African Journal of Higher Education* 22(4): 906–919.

World Bank (2010) *Financing Higher Education in Africa*. Washington DC: The World Bank.

Legislation

Decreto No 90/09, de 15 de Dezembro. Diário da República, I série, No 237 – estabelece as normas gerais reguladoras do subsistema de ensino superior.

Decreto No 2/09, de 29 de Abril. Diário da República, I série, No 70 – aprova o estatuto orgânico da Secretaria de Estado para o Ensino Superior.

Decreto Presidencial No 70/10, de 19 de Maio – Diário da República. I Série – No 93 – Aprova o Estatuto Orgânico do MESCT.

Decreto-lei No 7/09, de 12 de Maio. Diário da República, I série, No 87 – estabelece a Reorganização da rede de instituições de ensino superior e o redimensionamento da Universidade Agostinho Neto.

Resolução No 4/07, de 2 de Fevereiro. Diário da República, I série, No 15 – aprova as Linhas Mestras para a Melhoria da Gestão do Subsistema do Ensino Superior.

CHAPTER

3

CAPE VERDE

3.1 Country profile

The Republic of Cape Verde Islands is located in the mid-Atlantic Ocean, some 450 km off the west coast of Africa, and is Europe's closest tropical island chain. The archipelago includes ten islands, divided into the windward and leeward groups benefiting from stunning weather all year round. According to the Cape Verdean National Institute of Statistics (INE 2011), in 2010 the country had a population of about 570 000 inhabitants, but the majority of Cape Verdeans, almost 700 000 people, live abroad, in particular in Portugal, Angola, the Netherlands, France and the United States.

In terms of ethnicity, the majority of Cape Verdeans are *creole*, with both African and European ancestry. Portuguese is the official language of the country, but Creole, a mixture of indigenous African languages and European languages, is widely used in colloquial contexts. Administratively, the country is divided into 22 municipalities, and Praia is its capital city as well as its main economic, political and cultural centre.

A former Portuguese colony, Cape Verde became independent on 5 July 1975. The liberation movement was led by the PAIGC, the African Party for the Independence of Guinea and Cape Verde, whose leader, Amílcar Cabral, attempted unsuccessfully to unite Cape Verde with Guinea-Bissau, the other former Portuguese colony situated in West Africa.

From independence until 1990, the country was governed by a one-party political system, dominated by the PAICV. Responding to pressures for pluralist democracy, constitutional changes were brought about in the beginning of 1990, enabling opposition parties to participate in the electoral and political process. The first multi-party elections were held in 1990 and were won by an opposition party, the MPD (Movement for Democracy), under the leadership of António Mascarenhas Monteiro.

The legislative and presidential elections, held in 1995 and 1996 respectively, were again won by the MPD. The elections held in 2001 returned the PAICV and its presidential candidate, Pedro Pires, to power. Because of the fact that these government changes have occurred without violence, Cape Verde is considered an example of good governance and democratic change in Africa.

Compared to other Portuguese speaking African countries, Cape Verde ranks first in many political indicators, such as the Ibrahim Index of African governance, the press freedom index, the democratic index, the corruption perception index and e-government index on governance indicators (World Bank 2011). Constitutionally, Cape Verde is a representative, parliamentary republic. The president of the republic is the head of state, and the prime minister is the head of the government. The current president of Cape Verde is Jorge Carlos Fonseca and José Maria Neves is the prime minister. Jorge Carlos Fonseca won Cape Verde's presidential elections, beating his ruling party rival, Manuel Inocêncio Sousa in 2011. Mr Fonseca secured nearly 55% of the vote in run-off elections, compared to Mr Sousa's 45%. The two leaders contested the poll after President Pedro Pires stepped down at the end of his two terms.

Since the late 1990s, after the implementation of market-oriented policies, the economy of Cape Verde has experienced steady economic growth: its real GDP has grown at an annual average rate of around 7%. Without significant natural resources, the economy of the archipelago is service-oriented, with commerce, tourism, transport and public administration accounting for more than 70% of GDP. In 2010, the nominal GDP of Cape Verde was estimated to be USD 1.9 billion, and its per capita GDP was around USD 3 800 (*CIA World Factbook* 2010). The 2010 social indicators of the country are as follows: life expectancy, 71.7 years; literacy rate: 81.2%; child mortality rate: 24.6/1 000 births; Human Development Index, 0.534; population below poverty line: less than 30%; unemployment rate: 21% (*CIA World Factbook* 2010). Because of its strong economic performance and its social indicators, Cape Verde graduated from being one of the least developed countries to one of the middle income countries in 2007.

3.2 Background and historical context of higher education

When Cape Verde gained its independence in 1975, no HEI had yet been established. From 1975 to 1979, everyone wishing to obtain a university diploma had to travel abroad, in particular to Portugal, the Soviet Union and Eastern Europe, because of the strong relations the government of Cape Verde maintained with its former coloniser and with the socialist bloc. The first HEI, Escola de Formação de Professores de Ensino Secundário, was established in 1979 at Praia City, with the aim of training teachers. In 1984, the second HEI, Instituto de Formação Náutica, specialising in Marine Sciences, was established (Tolentino 2006, Vieira 2006, Rodriques 2005, Furtado 2008).

Higher education in Cape Verde is an extremely recent phenomenon. There was no university in the island until the establishment of Jean Piaget University in 2001, also the first private university in the country. Previously, the island had three small HEIs: the Instituto Superior de Educação (ISE), located in Praia and specialising in teacher training; Instituto Superior de Engenharia e Ciências do Mar (ISECMAR), in Mindelo; and the Instituto

Nacional de Investigação e Desenvolvimento Agrário (INIDA), in São Jorge dos Órgãos. The introduction of multi-party democracy and free-market economic policies in the early 1990s resulted in the expansion of higher education with the establishment of the Centro de Formação Agrária. Founded in 1992 in São Tiago Island, this HEI offers mainly Bachelors degrees in Agriculture and Forestry. The existing HEIs were also upgraded and expanded: in 1995, the Escola de Formação de Professores de Ensino Secundário became Instituto de Educação and, in 1996, the Escola de Formação Náutica became Instituto Superior de Engenharia e Ciências Marinhas (ISECMAR). Later, these entities were merged to form the first and only public university, the University of Cape Verde (UNI-CV).

3.3 Trends of expansion, diversification and differentiation

In 2010, Cape Verde had nine HEIs: eight private and one public (Table 3.1). As well as showing that Cape Verde's higher education is dominated by private institutions, Table 3.1 also indicates that the majority of HEIs were established towards the end of the 2000s. In 2010 about 10 000 students were enrolled in the nine HEIs (Table 3.2), the majority of whom are enrolled in private higher education institutions. In 2011, 4 549 students were enrolled in public institution as opposed to 7 220 in the private HEIs (MESCT 2011).

Institution	Type of institution	Accreditation	Legal decree of creation
Universidade de Cabo Verde – UNI-CV	Public	Full	Dec-Lei nº 53/2006
Universidade Jean Piaget – UNI-Piaget	Private	Full	Dec-Lei nº 12/2001
Instituto de Estudos Superiores Isidoro da Graça – IESIG	Private	Full	Resolução nº 12/2003
Instituto Superior de Ciências Jurídicas e Sociais – ISCJS	Private	Provisional	Dec-Lei nº 15/2009
Escola Internacional de Arte – M-EIA	Private	Provisional	Dec-Lei nº 16/2009
Universidade Lusófona de Cabo Verde DR. Baltazar Lopes da Silva – ULCV	Private	Provisional	Dec-Lei nº 17/2009
Universidade Intercontinental de Cabo Verde – UNICA	Private	Provisional	Dec-Lei nº 18/2009
Universidade de Santiago – US	Private	Provisional	Dec-Lei nº 19/2009
Instituto Superior de Ciências Económicas e Empresariais – ISCEE	Private	Provisional	Dec-Lei 52/98Dec-Lei nº 20/2009

Source: Minedu 2011

Table 3.2 Students enrolled in Cape Verdean higher education institutions in 2009/2010

Institution	Number of students
Universidade Pública de Cabo Verde (UNI-CV)	4 050
Universidade Jean Piaget de Cabo Verde (UNI-Piaget)	1 880
Instituto Superior de Ciências Económicas e Empresariais (ISCEE)	1 675
Instituto Superior de Ciências Jurídicas e Sociais (ISCJS)	897
Instituto de Estudos Superiores Isidoro da Graça (IESIG)	580
Universidade de Santiago (US)	545
Universidade Lusófona de Cabo Verde Baltazar Lopes da Silva (Lusófona)	332
Universidade Intercontinental de Cabo Verde (ÚNICA)	162
Mindeo Escola Internacional de Arte (M-EIA)	23
Total	10 144

Source: Statistical data produced by the Gabinete de Estudos e Planeamento, Ministério de Educação e Ensino Superior (www.minedu.gov.cv, estatísticas da educação)

Figures 3.1 and 3.2 as well as Table 3.3 show the enrolment trends in Cape Verdean higher education since early 2000s. Figure 3.1 shows a comparison of gross enrolments in higher education with those of other subsystems of education in Cape Verde.

Figures 3.1 and 3.2 depict the gross enrolment rates for primary, secondary and higher education subsectors. Higher education shows an exponential growth from the year 2001 to 2009. This increase is an indication of the emergence of new institutions, both public and private. From 2000 to 2005, the gross enrolment rates of primary, secondary and higher education increased continuously. But from 2005 onwards, the enrolment in primary and secondary education registered a decreasing trend, which contrasts with the rising trend of enrolment in higher education. Table 3.3 illustrates five main features of the higher education sector in Cape Verde.

Firstly, student enrolment increased in each HEI between 2003 and 2010. Secondly, the dominance of the private higher education sector accounts for more than half of the overall student enrolment in the country. Thirdly, some of the existing institutions changed their status and were upgraded. For instance, INAG and INIDA were transformed in 2008 and 2009, respectively; IES and ISECMAR were transformed into UNI-CV in 2008; ÚNICA, Lusófona and US were established in 2008 and are still operating. The only private HEI that has been in existence for a decade is UNI-Piaget, established in 2001.

Fourthly, despite being the only public HEI in the country, UNI-CV is the largest institution in terms of student enrolment, with about 4 050 students in 2010. UNI-Piaget is the second largest HEI in the country and the largest private HEI, with 1 880 enrolled students in 2010. The third largest HEI is ISCEE, with 1 675 enrolled students. The other institutions are relatively small, as they have fewer than 1 000 students. The smallest institution is M-EIA, with only 23 students. Fifthly, the different HEIs are referred to in three different terms. Five are *universities*, namely UNI-CV, UNI-Piaget, UNICA, US and Lusófona; three are *higher institutes*: IESIG, ISCEE, ISCJS; and only one is a *college*, M-EIA.

Figure 3.1 Gross enrolment rates 2000–2009

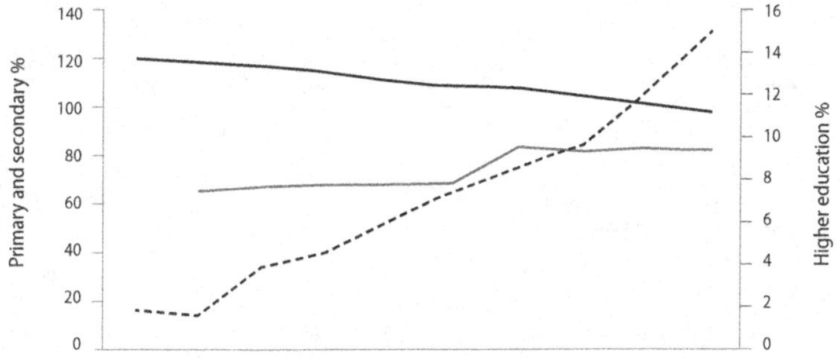

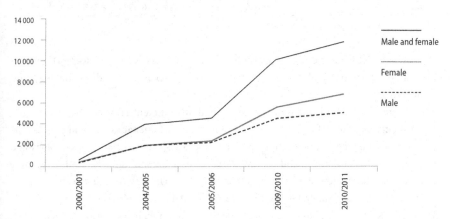

	2000	2001	2002	2003	2004	2005	2006	2007	2008	2009
Primary (6–11) ━━━━	120%	118%	117%	114%	111%	109%	107%	104%	101%	98%
Secondary (12–17) ━━━		65%	67%	68%	68%	68%	82%	81%	83%	81%
Higher education ━ ━ ━ ━	2%	2%	4%	4%	6%	7%	9%	10%	12%	15%

Source: Data collected from the Ministério de Educação e Ensino Superior and UNESCO, by Schwartzman (2011)

Figure 3.2 below shows the gross enrolment rates by gender from 2002/2001 to 2010/2011. Both gender categories show a growing tendency. Females (F) however show faster growth from 2005, compared to males (M). In 2012, both male and female enrolments had reached almost 12 000 students.

Figure 3.2 Gross enrolment rates 2000/2001–2010

```
14 000
12 000                                                    ━━━━━━━━
10 000                                                    Male and female
 8 000
 6 000                                                    ━━━━━━━━
 4 000                                                    Female
 2 000
     0                                                    - - - - - - -
       2000/2001  2004/2005  2005/2006  2009/2010  2010/2011   Male
```

Source: MED, MESCI 2012

Table 3.3 Evolution of higher education institutions

Institution	Academic year					
	2003/ 2004	2004/ 2005	2006/ 2007	2007/ 2008	2008/ 2009	2009/ 2010
Universidade Jean Piaget (UNI-Piaget)	913	1 248	1 494	1 671	2 129	1 880
Instituto Superior de Educação (ISE)	989	1 250	1 706	2 143	–	–
Instituto Superior de Enginharia e Ciências do Mar (ISECMAR)	425	577	635	640	–	–
Universidade Pública de Cabo Verde (UNI-CV)	–	–	–	–	3 245	4 050
Instituto de Estudos Superiores Isidoro da Graça (IESIG)	440	464	570	721	749	580
Instituto Superior de Ciências Económicas e Empresariais (ISCEE)	269	299	613	795	1 034	1 675
Instituto Nacional de Investigação e Desenvolvimento Agrário (INIDA)	–	48	44	44	44	–
Instituto Nacional de Administração e Gestão (INAG)	–	–	–	103	–	–
Mindelo escola Internacional de Arte (M-EIA)	–	25	–	–	19	23
Instituto Superior de Ciências Jurídicas e Sociais (ISCJS)	–	–	227	380	537	897
Universidade Lusófona de Cabo Verde Baltasar Lopes da Silva (Lusófona)	–	–	–	161	266	332
Universidade Intercontinental de Cabo Verde (ÚNICA)	–	–	–	–	107	162
Universidade de Santiago (US)	–	–	–	–	335	545
Total	3 036	3 911	5 289	6 658	8 465	10 144

Source: Ministério de Educação e Ensino Superior

The different HEIs offer different academic programmes (see Tables 3.4 to 3.14), ranging from arts, humanities and social sciences to business sciences, health, technology and engineering.

According to the academic programmes offered, the different HEIs can be divided into two distinct categories. The first category includes HEIs that offer academic and professional programmes, ranging from arts, humanities and social sciences to business, technology and engineering. The former ISE and ISECMAR, merged in 2008 to form the UNI-CV, can be integrated in the first category, as well as the IESIG and US. The second category consists of specialised HEIs, namely ISCEE, INAG, INIDA, M-EIA, Lusófona, ISCJS and ÚNICA. ISCEE, INAG, ISCJS and Lusófona offer academic programmes in law, business sciences and social service; M-EIA specialises in arts and design, UNICA in health sciences and INIDA in agricultural and environmental sciences.

The majority of these HEIs offer Bachelors and Honours degrees. ISE and ISECMAR were the first HEIs to introduce Masters degrees in the academic year 2006/2007. When ISE and ISECMAR were transformed into UNI-CV, the previously introduced Masters programmes were maintained, and new Masters degrees were introduced. Apart from UNI-CV, two private HEIs also offer Masters academic programmes: IESIG and ISCEE. But the overall number of students attending Masters academic programmes is fairly small, compared to those attending Bachelors degrees. In 2010, the share of enrolment in Masters programmes, in comparison with the overall number of students, was as follows: IESIG: 41/580; ISCEE: 29/1 675; UNI-CV: 350/4 050. Only two HEIs offered PhD programmes. UNI-Piaget was the first institution to offer a PhD programme in personal development and social intervention. With only eight students, this programme was discontinued in 2009. In 2010, UNI-CV introduced a PhD programme in social sciences, with ten students.

Table 3.4 Academic programmes offered by IESIG

Degrees	Academic programmes	Academic year					
		2003/ 2004	2004/ 2005	2006/ 2007	2007/ 2008	2008/ 2009	2009/ 2010
Bachelors/ Bachelor Honours	Sociology	71	63	72	64	53	17
	Psychology	98	84	127	102	97	84
	History	56	50	68	79	67	26
	Hotel and Tourism Management	62	109	123	124	120	84
	Computer Science Applied to Management	70	87	52	45	49	29
	English Studies	44	38	42	42	29	30
	French Studies	0	0	–	–	–	–
	Cape Verdean and Portuguese Studies	37	30	30	13	21	11
	Management	–	–	–	132	148	102
	Law	–	–	–	120	124	86
	Nursing	–	–	–	–	–	70
Masters	Pedagogic Supervision	–	–	–	–	23	23
	Social Sciences	–	–	–	–	18	18
Total		440	464	570	721	749	580

Table 3.5 Academic programmes offered by ISCEE

Degrees	Academic programmes	Academic year					
		2003/ 2004	2004/ 2005	2006/ 2007	2007/ 2008	2008/ 2009	2009/ 2010
Bachelors/ Bachelor Honours	Accounting	238	268	311	378	463	792
	Business Management	31	31	156	249	294	608
	Financial Management	–	–	119	141	186	65
Masters	Management			27	27	29	29
Total		269	299	613	795	1 034	1 675

Table 3.6 Academic programmes offered by INAG

Degrees	Academic programmes	Academic year					
		2003/ 2004	2004/ 2005	2006/ 2007	2007/ 2008	2008/ 2009	2009/ 2010
Bachelors/ Bachelor Honours	Administration and Management	–	–	–	74	–	–
	Secretariat and Public Relations	–	–	–	29	–	–
Total		–	–	–	103	–	–

Table 3.7 Academic programmes offered by ISE/IESCMAR/UNI-CV

HEIs	Degrees	Academic programmes	Academic year					
			ISE/ISECMAR				UNI-CV	
			2003/ 2004	2004/ 2005	2006/ 2007	2007/ 2008	2008/ 2009	2009/ 2010
ISE	Bachelors/ Bachelor Honours	Physics/Chemistry	88	53	6	–	–	22
		Pedagogy/Pedagogical Supervision	–	68	67	24	–	80
		Physical Education	49	43	76	70	61	95
		Physics	–	22	69	57	47	30
		Chemistry	–	23	70	94	62	38
		Natural Sciences	16	–	–	–	–	–
		History	92	111	70	98	82	69
		Biology	65	88	114	139	148	177
		Mathematics	110	87	136	124	105	107
		Philosophy	60	56	89	116	70	116
		English Studies	125	143	151	173	125	55
		French Studies	100	125	91	156	110	93
		Cape Verdean and Portuguese studies	137	186	208	136	136	129
		Child Education	–	–	163	144	134	–
		Educational Sciences	–	–	–	96	78	142
		Social Sciences	–	–	–	59	124	171
		Modern Arts	–	–	57	45	40	
		Languages, Literature, Culture	–	–	–	–	156	240
		Geology	21	48	31	29	05	–
		Planning and Management	61	57	–	–	–	–
		Geography	49	108	133	210	209	222
		Statistics and Management of ICT	–	–	–	29	61	78
		ICT	16	12	02	80	62	47
		Nursing	–	–	–	–	35	128

Table 3.7 Academic programmes offered by ISE/IESCMAR/UNI-CV (cont.)

HEIs	Degrees	Academic programmes	ISE/ISECMAR 2003/ 2004	ISE/ISECMAR 2004/ 2005	ISE/ISECMAR 2006/ 2007	ISE/ISECMAR 2007/ 2008	UNI-CV 2008/ 2009	UNI-CV 2009/ 2010
	Masters	Portuguese Teaching	–	–	9	–	–	–
		African Studies	–	–	–	24	–	–
		Special Education	–	–	–	30	30	–
		Educational Sciences			–	–	–	18
		Social Sciences	–	–	30	31	60	20
		Electronic Engineering	–	–	27	27	42	15
		Applied Mathematics (for Engineers)	–	–	13	15	13	–
		Territory/development management	–	–	–	24	24	25
		Patrimony and Development	–	–	–	24	24	24
		Geographical Information Systems	–	–	–	–	24	40
		Public Administration	–	–	–	–	31	49
		Public Security	–	–	–	–	–	25
		Law and Municipality Governance	–	–	–	–	–	18
		Finance	–	–	–	–	34	34
	PhD	Social Sciences	–	–	–	–	–	10
CMAR	Bachelor/ Bachelor honours	Planning/Management Maritime Transports	45	60	103	130	–	31
		Training of Teachers of Engineering	–	68	–	–	–	–
		Business Management	–	–	–	–	130	201
		Public Relations and Secretariat	–	–	–	–	87	193
		Communication and Multimedia	–	–	–	–	49	–
		Applied Mathematics	54	65	69	77	130	107
		Marine Biology and Fishery	43	43	46	50	55	55
		Civil Engineering	58	59	91	30	154	249
		Mechanical Engineering	53	91	81	40	98	43
		Electronic Engineering	–	–	–	–	31	31
		Electro-technical Engineering	–	–	–	–	–	25
		Telecommunication Engineering	48	57	69	69	33	27

Table 3.7   Academic programmes offered by ISE/IESCMAR/UNI-CV (cont.)

HEIs	Degrees	Academic programmes	Academic year					
			ISE/ISECMAR				UNI-CV	
			2003/ 2004	2004/ 2005	2006/ 2007	2007/ 2008	2008/ 2009	2009/ 2010
CMAR		Computer Science Engineering and Automation	67	77	88	55	36	28
		Electronic and Electric Engineering	47	50	69	60	64	29
		Computer Science and Computer Engineering	–	–	–	–	–	138
		Biochemical Engineering	–	–	–	–	23	84
		Naval Engineering	–	–	19	14	29	–
	Masters	Energy	–	–	–	15	15	30
		Mechanical Engineering	–	–	–	17	17	17
		Sea Resources and Coast Management	–	–	–	17	17	17
		Agronomy and natural resources	–	–	–	–	–	18
CEPS (short-term professional capacity-building Training Programmes)		Building Management and Supervision	–	–	–	–	48	38
		Maintenance of Hospital and Hotel Equipment	–	–	–	–	42	38
		Accounting Practices	–	–	–	–	66	65
		Bio-diagnosis	–	–	–	–	36	38
		Topography and Computer-assisted Design	–	–	–	–	40	33
		Micro-irrigation and New Technologies for Agricultural Production	–	–	–	–	–	29
		Phytology/Zoology	–	–	–	–	–	31
		Social and Community Development	–	–	–	–	–	90
		Public Administration Procedures	–	–	–	–	–	21
		Installation and Maintenance of Renewable Energy and Equipment	–	–	–	–	–	25
		Installation and Maintenance of Computer Science Network and Systems	–	–	–	–	–	25
Total			989	1 250	1 706	2 143	3 245	4 050

NB: In 2008/2009, ISE and ISECMAR were merged to form UNI-CV

Table 3.8 Academic programmes offered by Lusófona

Degrees	Academic programmes	Academic year					
		2003/ 2004	2004/ 2005	2006/ 2007	2007/ 2008	2008/ 2009	2009/ 2010
Bachelor/ Bachelor Honours	Account Administration Auditing	–	–	–	20	31	26
	Hotel/Tourism Management	–	–	–	32	38	36
	Law	–	–	–	33	53	65
	Business Management	–	–	–	40	58	71
	Communication Sciences	–	–	–	36	53	83
	Social Service	–	–	–	–	33	51
Total		–	–	–	161	266	332

Source: Author's field work 2012

Table 3.9 Academic programmes offered by UNI-Piaget

Degrees	Academic programmes	Academic year					
		2003/ 2004	2004/ 2005	2006/ 2007	2007/ 2008	2008/ 2009	2009/ 2010
Bachelor/ Bachelor Honours	Architecture	22	33	13	89	148	155
	Communication Sciences	73	121	29	146	179	156
	Educational Sciences	96	122	39	215	262	176
	Economics and Management	222	248	357	401	475	394
	Civil Engineering	11	116	17	69	101	90
	Nursing	28	–	–	–	–	–
	Social service	–	–	–	66	79	67
	Eng. of Systems and Computer Science	69	94	26	172	268	248
	Hotel and Tourism Management	31	17	4	16	27	23
	Computer Science applied to Management	66	83	25	116	129	87
	Public Administration and Local Governance	–	–	–	17	34	80
	Law	–	–	–	16	47	64
	Psychology	111	154	48	–	–	–
	Sociology	117	135	35	77	57	52
	Pharmacy	19	27	16	38	30	43
	Physiotherapy	34	39	9	26	34	23
	Clinical Analysis and Public Health	–	5		42	62	72
	Biology	–	–	–	145	176	150
	Portuguese Teaching (Master)	6	6	–	–	–	–
	Mathematics/Mathematics Teaching	–	–	12	9	2	–
	Advertising and Marketing	–	–	9	–	–	–
PhD	Personal Development and Social Intervention	8	8	8	8	8	–
Total		913	1 248	1 494	1 671	2 129	1 880

Source: Author's field work 2012

Table 3.10 Academic programmes offered by INIDA

		Academic year					
Degrees	Academic programmes	2003/ 2004	2004/ 2005	2006/ 2007	2007/ 2008	2008/ 2009	2009/ 2010
Bachelor/	Environmental Engineering	–	28	29	29	29	–
Bachelor Honours	Rural Engineering	–	20	15	15	15	–
Total		–	48	44	44	44	–

Source: Author's field work, 2012

Table 3.11 Academic programmes offered by M-EIA

		Academic year					
Degrees	Academic programmes	2003/ 2004	2004/ 2005	2006/ 2007	2007/ 2008	2008/ 2009	2009/ 2010
Bachelor/	Visual Arts	–	25	–	–	7	6
Bachelor Honours	Design	–	–	–	–	12	17
Total		–	25	–	–	19	23

Source: Author's field work 2012

Table 3.12 Academic programmes offered by ISCJS

		Academic year					
Degrees	Academic programmes	2003/ 2004	2004/ 2005	2006/ 2007	2007/ 2008	2008/ 2009	2009/ 2010
Bachelor/	Law	–	–	159	256	356	464
Bachelor Honours	Social Service	–	–	68	124	181	433
Total		–	–	227	380	537	897

Source: Author's field work 2012

Table 3.13 Academic programmes offered by UNICA

		Academic year					
Degrees	Academic programmes	2003/ 2004	2004/ 2005	2006/ 2007	2007/ 2008	2008/ 2009	2009/ 2010
Bachelor/	Nursing	–	–	–	–	39	68
Bachelor Honours	Pharmacy	–	–	–	–	8	16
	Physical Education and Sports	–	–	–	–	37	21
	Physiotherapy	–	–	–	–	7	23
	Clinical Analysis and Public Health	–	–	–	–	16	34
Total		–	–	–	–	107	162

Source: Author's field work 2012

Table 3.14 Academic programmes offered by US

Degrees	Academic programmes	Academic year					
		2003/ 2004	2004/ 2005	2006/ 2007	2007/ 2008	2008/ 2009	2009/ 2010
Bachelor/ Bachelor Honours	Geography	–	–	–	–	44	48
	History	–	–	–	–	31	26
	Sociology	–	–	–	–	62	82
	Philosophy	–	–	–	–	20	16
	French Studies	–	–	–	–	20	39
	Educational Sciences	–	–	–	–	–	32
	SSPP	–	–	–	–	–	62
	Nursing	–	–	–	–	–	19
	Accountancy	–	–	–	–	–	37
	Business Management	–	–	–	–	75	73
	Economics	–	–	–	–	52	73
	ICT	–	–	–	–	31	38
Total		–	–	–	–	335	545

Source: Author's field work 2012

The academic programmes offered in Cape Verde's HEIs are administered by an academic staff whose academic qualifications are hardly beyond the Masters degree. Table 3.15 overleaf shows the number of academic staff and their respective qualification for each HEI. In 2003 there were 542 university lecturers, 281 of whom had a Bachelors degree, 101 a Masters degree, and only 16 a PhD. In 2010, the overall number of university lecturers had increased to 915 (509 with a Bachelors degree, 359 with a Masters and 57 with a PhD).

In 2010, UNI-CV had the highest number of lecturers: 263 (121 Bachelors, 117 Masters and 25 PhDs). Even though, the largest group of UNI-CV's academic staff held a Bachelors degree, as it was the case in other four private HEIs, namely UNICA, UNI-Piaget, Lusófona and M-EIA. Only two HEIs had the largest group of lecturers holding a Masters degree: ISCEE with 85 Masters, 72 Bachelors and 3 PhDs; US with 36 Masters, 18 Bachelors and 5 PhDs. Lecturers holding a PhD degree are the smallest group in all Cape Verdean HEIs.

Table 3.16 shows the academic staff who worked in the year 2010/2011 in Cape Verdean HEIs. A total of 1 259 lectures worked in both public and private HEIs in Cape Verde, with 739 working in private and 520 in public. In terms of their academic qualifications, the majority (59.3%) hold a graduate level, Masters, Doctoral and Postdoctorate. There is one important difference between public and private institutions regarding the training of academic staff. In private institutions about 48% of lecturers hold a graduate degree, while those in public institutions at this level represent only 31%. There is a significant percentage of holders of Masters degrees, whether in private or in public schools. The biggest difference lies in the Doctoral degree, with 24.6% for the public and 6.4% for private. The percentage of academic staff with a Postdoctorate is 1.9% in public institutions.

Table 3.15 Number and qualifications of academic staff of HEIs

Academic categories	Year	UNI-Piaget	ISE	ISECMAR	IESIG	ISCEE	INIDA	MEIA	ISCJS	INAG	Lusófona	UNICA	UNI-CV	US	Total
Professors'/ lecturers' academic qualifications	Bachelors and Bachelors Honours degrees														
	03/04	77	50	78	52	24	–	–	–	–	–	–	–	–	281
	04/05	111	87	48	39	31	–	7	–	–	2	–	–	–	325
	05/06	–	–	–	–	–	–	–	–	–	–	–	–	–	–
	06/07	124	75	89	34	29	6	–	3	–	–	–	–	–	360
	07/08	131	138	71	62	26	6	–	5	17	20	–	–	–	476
	08/09	129	–	–	66	37	6	4	3	–	42	14	148	11	460
	09/10	114	–	–	85	72	–	10	10	–	50	29	121	18	509
	Masters and Postgraduate degrees														
	03/04	36	33	11	12	9	–	–	–	–	–	–	–	–	101
	04/05	34	49	12	15	15	–	–	–	–	–	–	–	–	125
	05/06	–	–	–	–	–	–	–	–	–	–	–	–	–	–
	06/07	59	33	24	23	43	4	–	6	–	–	–	–	–	192
	07/08	65	83	13	16	57	4	–	15	11	4	–	–	–	268
	08/09	67	–	–	19	89	4	1	20	–	9	10	108	25	325
	09/10	62	–	–	12	85	–	2	22	–	13	10	117	36	359
	Doctorate degrees														
	03/04	8	4	1	3	–	–	–	–	–	–	–	–	–	16
	04/05	16	13	1	6	–	–	1	–	–	–	–	–	–	37
	05/06	–	–	–	–	–	–	–	–	–	–	–	–	–	–
	06/07	11	8	–	2	–	15	–	2	–	–	–	–	–	38
	07/08	7	14	–	4	2	15	–	2	1	3	–	–	–	48
	08/09	13	–	–	5	5	15	1	3	–	2	4	17	5	65
	09/10	7	–	–	5	3	–	4	2	–	5	4	25	5	57

Source: Field work 2012, MESCI 2012

Table 3.16 Percentage distribution of academic staff by qualifications

Institution	Post-doc	PhD	MA/MSc	Postgrad.	BA Hons./ BSc	BA	Total
Public	10	128	221	1	160	0	520
	1.9%	24.6%	42.5%	0.2%	30.8%	0.0%	
Private	–	47	294	46	351	1	739
	0.0%	6.4%	39.8%	6.2%	47.5%	0.1%	
Total	10	175	515	47	511	1	1 259
	0.8%	13.9%	40.9%	3.7%	40.6%	0.1%	

Source: MESCI 2012

3.4 Changes in higher education governance

Before 1990 there was no law regulating Cape Verde's system of education in general, and the higher education subsystem in particular. From 1975 to 1990 the functioning of educational institutions was regulated by specific decrees, such as Decree 70/79 through which Escola de Formação de Professores de Ensino Secundário was established. The first education law, Law 103/III/1990, was promulgated on 26 December 1990. This law was designed to regulate the whole education system, including the higher education subsystem.

Subsection IV of the law is especially concerned with higher education: it defines the scope, objectives, academic degrees and other honorary degrees, the conditions for access and the different types of HEIs. The law divides higher education into two different kinds, the university or academic higher education and polytechnic higher education (Article 31). This division corresponds to three different types of HEIs defined by the law, namely universities, colleges and higher institutes (Article 43). Universities are both general and specialised institutions, but higher schools and higher institutes are only specialised institutions, at least in legal terms. Another aspect of Law 103/III/1990 worth mentioning is the fact that it sets four university academic degrees, namely *bacharelato* (BA), *licenciatura* (BA Honours), *mestrado* (MA) and *doutoramento* (PhD).

Law 103/III/1990 was altered in 1999 (Basic Law of the Education System), particularly in the articles concerning higher education. However, the changes were more about wording than content. The only new aspect that deserves to be mentioned was the blurring of the differences between universities and higher institutes and schools. While Law 103/III/1990 was clearer in attributing to the universities mainly a scientific-academic role and to higher institutes and schools a professional-technical role, in the altered version these differences are difficult to discern.

Law 103/III/1990 and its altered version barely mention private HEIs. Law 103/III/1990 (Article 76, 6) only states that the criteria for the functioning of private HEIs will be specified in a specific decree. However, the Estatuto do Ensino Privado (Private Education Statute), approved by Decree 17/96 of 3 July, did not concern higher education. The absence of a law for regulating private HEIs was maintained until October 2005, the year in which the government approved Decree 65/2005 of 24 October, which states the rules for the creation and functioning of private HEIs. During the period of non-existence of legal instruments regulating private HEIs, according to Varela (2008) the government used other mechanisms to allow the creation and functioning of HEIs. In order to authorise the creation of UNI-Piaget, in 2001, the government used a legislative procedure, by promulgating, on 17 May 2001, Decree 11 and 12/2001.

To authorise IESIG, the government used an administrative procedure: by resolution 12/2003, of 9 June, the council of ministers authorised the Graça Empreendimentos to open IESIG. Decree 65/2005 was the first legal instrument defining and specifying the conditions through which private entities should create and maintain HEIs. The provisional nature of Decree 65/2005 led to the approval of Decree 32/2007 of 3 September, which institutes definitely the Private Higher Education Statute. This Statute considers private HEIs to be those administered by singular, cooperative or other private collective entities.

Despite their public nature defined by the Law 103/III/1990, the public HEIs in Cape Verde can be put under private administration, similarly to the private HEIs. As a matter of fact, the Law 97/V/99 defines the basic principles of private management of public HEIs. These principles include:

(i) the possibility, ordered by a government resolution, of the public HEI being managed by private collective entities from the business sector;
(ii) public institutions can be managed by a private entities as long as there is a contract between the parties; and
(iii) the public entities are obliged to support the private management entities, in terms of equipment, installations, training, scientific research and obligation of delivering education services under the same conditions as a public higher education system.

Apart from legislation, Cape Verde has institutional governance boards that regulate, coordinate and supervise the higher education system. By 2009, before the founding of the ministry of education and higher education, higher education was governed, coordinated and controlled by specific structures within the ministry of education and human resources development. After the closure of the ministry of education and human resources development, two ministries were established: the ministry of education and sports, and the ministry of education and higher education.

Higher education is currently coordinated and supervised by the ministry of education and higher education, precisely by the general directorate of higher education and science. The general directorate of higher education and science has three main advising boards: the Council for Quality Assurance, the Service for Higher Education Access, and a unit responsible for science and technology. Because of the dominance of private HEIs and of the autonomous nature of higher education in Cape Verde, the general directorate for higher education and sciences is more a coordinating body than a governing body, as stated by Schwartzman (2011). More recently, a new higher education governance structure was set up after the election held in 2011. The new structure brought higher education, science and innovation under the same ministry. However, higher education still is coordinated by the general directorate of higher education.

3.5   Financing higher education

In Cape Verde, there are two mechanisms of financing higher education, namely public and private financing. Public financing is provided by the government through state subsidies, and private financing by the students. As the only public HEI in the country, UNI-CV is the sole institution that receives direct funding support from the government. But as the amount allocated is not sufficient to cover the overall institution's costs, UNI-CV has a tuition system to address its budget deficit.

According to Schwartzman (2011: 16), 40% of UNI-CV's budget comes from the government and the other part from the tuition fees paid by students. Schwartzman (2011) states that in 2011, monthly fees in UNI-CV were between 9 000 and 11 000 *escudos cabo-verdianos* (ECV) (USD 120–150).

3.5.1 Tuitions fees and cost-sharing

The financing of the private HEIs is completely dependent on the tuition and other fees paid by students. UNI-Piaget is the private HEI with the highest monthly fees, ranging from 16 000 up to 20 000 ECV (USD 270). Monthly fees at other private HEI are: IESIG: 15 000 ECV; ISCEE: 16 000 to 17 000 ECV; US: 14 000 to 18 000 ECV; ISCJS: 16 000 to 18 000 ECV (Schwartzman 2011).

In order to determine whether these monthly fees are affordable or not, data on average salaries paid in the country is necessary. As it is difficult to get information on the salaries paid in different sectors across the country, information on salaries paid in public administration and to domestic workers may suffice to determine the affordability of the fees applied by the HEIs.

The selection of public administration as a reference is justified by the fact that it is a significant employer in the country; and the selection of domestic workers is based on the fact that these workers receive one of the lowest salaries in the country. The average monthly salary paid to domestic workers was around 10 000 ECV in 2009. Regarding public administration employees, the lowest monthly salary was 13 745 ECV in 2009, the average monthly salary paid to general public servants and senior top staff was 37 500 ECV and 53 000 ECV, respectively (UNTC-CS *et al.* 2009).

With the monthly salary they receive, domestic workers and civil servants in the lowest salary rank cannot even afford to pay the monthly fees of UNI-CV. The comparison between salaries and fees enables one to conclude that only middle and upper income social groups can afford to attend higher education in Cape Verde. However, low income groups may also enter the university through scholarships granted by the ministry of higher education and the Education and Training Fund (Fundo de Apoio à Educação e Formação), which provides support to study both in the country and abroad (Schwartzman 2011).

3.5.2 Shifting from international to local scholarships

Few, if any, countries have experienced emigration as extensively as Cape Verde. The Diaspora outnumbers the resident population, and virtually every family has emigrant members. The importance of migration makes the country particularly vulnerable to the tightening of immigration policy in Europe and North America. Recent decades have been marked by declining emigration, increasing population growth and considerable migration pressure (Carling 2002).

According to Carling (2002), traditionally Cape Verdeans would study abroad for their higher education degrees, rather than in their own country. The geographical dispersion of the Cape Verdean islands, the small size of its population and the historical migration tradition of Cape Verdeans due to the unfavourable condition of their land, has created a tradition of training mostly overseas. Carling (2001, 2002a, 2000b) argues that cultural explanations of the aspiration to emigrate can also be found in Cape Verdeans' perception of their own nation. Even with a standard of living that is among the highest in Africa, the notion of Cape Verde as a place of inescapable poverty is pervasive. The persistent lack of rain, the smallness and remoteness of the country, and the constant exposure to European and American lifestyles through contact with emigrants all add to this. Indeed, much of the wealth that is visible in the form of fancy cars and large houses comes from working abroad. For many years there has been an inadequate supply of higher education in the islands. The argument for the reluctance to establish HEIs was that small islands, with their small-scale economies and dispersed population, would represent higher investments costs in transportation and communication (Fragosouyhjj 2005).

3.5.2.1 Study abroad and the desire to emigrate
The desire to study and work abroad is common in Cape Verde. The government's quarterly employment surveys include a question about the wish to emigrate, and typical results show that more than half of the respondents have this wish (with fluctuations over time and between islands) (Carling 2002). According to Barros (2012) the same trend applies to studies. Most Cape Verdeans, even those from poor socio-economic back grounds, will work hard to save some money to send their children to study abroad. Data shows that being unemployed, having relatives abroad, and receiving remittances are factors that contribute to the wish to emigrate. However, the percentage of prospective emigrants declines markedly with age and with the level of education. The explosion of secondary education and the growth of the higher education private sector have had an impact on the migration trend. For Barros (2012) the establishment of UNI-CV, the sole public HEI, attracted many Cape Verdeans who would otherwise have opted to study abroad. However, study abroad is still the preference of the upper middle class.

For Carling (2002) the widespread desire to emigrate cannot be explained exclusively by economic or demographic factors. The idea of emigration and return as a path to prosperity is a deeply rooted aspect of Cape Verdean society. When talking about their wish to emigrate, most Cape Verdeans relate to emigration as a 'package' of expected events: going abroad, working hard, returning with savings and securing a better future at the place of origin. As in most cases, the original intention to return often fades over time. To a large extent, Cape Verdeans studying abroad and returning to the country have not only supplied the needs for highly skilled personnel in the island, but have also benefitted from the status that overseas study has brought them.

3.5.2.2 Local scholarships
In 2007, for the first time, the number of Cape Verdeans studying on the island exceeded that of those studying abroad. By 2010 there were more than 10 000 students in Cape Verdean institutions and about 6 000 studying abroad (Neves 2010). According to Neves (2010) about 5 000 young people are recipients of scholarships to pursue their higher education studies in Cape Verde as well as abroad, representing an investment of about 500 000 ECV. Fiscal

measures were put in place to promote access to higher education, and the government is working to develop an integrated system of scholarships, especially to support the poorest households, and to ensure access to finance for young people who want to develop business initiatives. Figure 3.3 shows that local scholarships increased from 230 in 2007/2008 to 246 in 2008/2009, and to 312 in 2009/2010. In 2009/2010, the Education and Training Fund supported 1 022 local scholarships and 1 300 overseas scholarships.

Figure 3.3 Number of scholarships awarded in local HEIs, 2006–2011

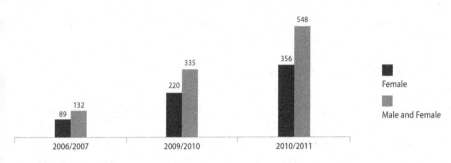

Source: MESCI 2012

3.6 Quality assurance

Until 2012 there were no (external) quality assurance mechanisms in the Cape Verdean higher education system. Legislation permitting the establishment and running of new higher institution is the only bureaucratic mechanism to assure minimum quality in Cape Verdean higher education. Most of this legislation dates back to 2007 and was specifically designed to address the growing private higher education sector (República de Cabo Verde 2007, Correia e Silva 2012, interview).

Prior to that, authorisation for the establishment and running was granted on a provisional basis without significant prerequisites. In 2009, for the first time government decided to establish some sort of external evaluation procedure to assess the quality of the two main private institutions in the country, UNI-Piaget and the Instituto de Estudos Superiores Isidoro da Graça (Brito A 2012, interview).

An external commission comprised of Portuguese academics used institutional self-evaluations reports as well as institutional documents combined with site visits to assess and validate the institutional evaluation.

The external evaluation report made very specific recommendations to both institutions. For UNI-Piaget, the external evaluators recommended that the institution should implement the views and ideas expressed in their strategic plan for institutional development. For instance, the commission noted that the qualifications of the academic staff of the university are still insufficient in spite of the substantial effort being done for providing them with Masters and Doctoral degrees. It noted also that the working contracts, renewable annually, are not compatible with the goal of staff stability (Schwartzman 2011). Overall, the evaluators gave recommendations pointing out the need to strengthen the institution's academic staff.

For IESIG, the evaluators found a huge gap between the views and ideas expressed in the institution's strategic plan and its limited implementation in terms of material resources and academic staff qualifications. The external evaluation process was a unique experience. The evaluators had no mandate to sanction the institutions if they found threats to quality. The standards and procedures applied by them were based on their own experience in Portugal.

From the interview with the Cape Verdean higher education authorities and officials, I was assured that Cape Verde is on its way to establishing a comprehensive quality assurance mechanism drawing from the experiences of European countries such as Portugal, as well as from its African counterparts (Correia e Silva 2012, interview).

3.7 ICT in higher education

ICT infrastructure in Cape Verde can best be described as improving, but still faces major challenges. According Agyeman (2007), Cape Verde has made significant strides in the implementation of ICTs in education. The drawback of doing so has been the exorbitant cost of internet connection and services owing to the monopoly maintained by Cabo Verde Telecom. Furthermore, the availability of the technology in terms of usability by the general population is limited to two islands where cyber cafés have been established by private companies nearly to the exclusion of the others. The 30% of the population living below the poverty line may never be able to access such facilities, and another 12 000 families may never enjoy such communication because the terrain makes it impossible for electric power to be extended to them using traditional means. The country's objective of using information channels to introduce new educational technologies was articulated in the country's Education for All (EFA) plan and was reinforced by the Education Strategic Plan for 2003–2013, which recommends the establishment, strengthening, and replication of information and communication networks in the education system.

REFERENCES

Agyeman T (2007) ICT in Education in Cape Verde. *Survey of ICT and Education in Africa: Cape Verde Country Report.* Available at: http://ddp-ext.worldbank.org/EdStats/CPVpro07. pdf [accessed March 2012].

Carling J (2002a) Cape Verde: Towards the End of Emigration? In *Migration Information Source. Fresh Thought, Authoritative Data, Global Reach.* Available at: http://www. migrationinformation.org/feature/print.cfm?ID=68 [accessed April 2012].

Carling J (2002b) Migration in the Age of Involuntary Immobility: Theoretical reflections and Cape Verdean experiences. *Journal of Ethnic and Migration Studies* 28 (1): 5–42.

Carling J (2001) Aspiration and Ability in International Migration: Cape Verdean experiences of mobility and immobility. *Dissertations and Theses* 2001(5). Centre for Development and the Environment, University of Oslo.

Fragoso M (2005) Universidades Públicas em Pequenos Estados Insulares. Unpublished Report.

Furtado EML (2006) Auditoria Interna como Factor de Promoção da Qualidade do Serviço Educativo – sua aplicação no controlo dos sumários na Universidade Jean Piaget de Cabo Verde. Praia. (unpublished document). Available at: http://bdigital.cv.unipiaget.org:8080/ jspui/bitstream/123456789/90/1/Auditoria%20interna%20como%20factor%20de%20 promo%C3%A7%C3%A3o%20da%20qualidade.pdf [accessed 17August 2011].

MINEDU (2011) *Statistical Data Produced by the Gabinete de Estudos e Planeamento, Ministério de Educação e Ensino Superior.* Available at: www.minedu.gov.cv [accessesd 20 August 2011].

INE (2011) *Estatísticas da educação.* Available at: http://www.ine.cv/ [accessed 5 August 2011].

Neves JM (2010) *Construindo a Prosperidade para Todos.* Discurso do Estado da Nação pronunciado por sua excelência o primeiro-ministro, Dr José Maria Neves, na assembleia nacional 30 July 2010.

República de Cabo Verde (2007) Estatuto do Ensino Superior Particular e Cooperativo. Ministros Boletim Oficial.

Rodrigues JC (2005) A relação Pesquisa e Desenvolvimento Humano no Ensino Superior em Cabo Verde. Praia. Trabalho de estudantes do doutoramento da Universidade Jean Piaget. Unpublished. Available at: http://bdigital.unipiaget.cv:8080/jspui/bitstream/12345-6789/75/1/A%20Rela%C3%A7%C3%A3o%20Pesquisa%20e%20Desenvolvimento%20 Humano.pdf [accessed 18 August 2011].

Schwartzman S (2011) The Growth of Higher Education and Its Potential Contribution to Economic Growth in Cape Verde. A paper prepared at the request of the World Bank. Available at: http://www.schwartzman.org.br/simon/caboverde.pdf [accessed 20 August 2011].

UNTC-CS and Fundação Paz e Solidariedade Serafin Aliaga (2009) *Estudo sobre a criação do salário mínimo em Cabo Verde.* Praia. Available at: http://blog.ccoo.es/gallery/26/ Sal%E1rio%20M%EDnimo.pdf [accessed 20 August 2011].

Varela B (2008) *Breve Reflexão Sobre o Ensino Privado em Cabo Verde*. Available at: http:// unicv.academia.edu/BartolomeuVarela/Papers/473146/O_ensino_privado_em_Cabo_ Verde [accessed 4 August 201].

Vieira FHRA (2008) Investigação e Ensino Superior: A relação entre a investigação na pós-graduação e a docência no ensino superior na cidade da Praia. Praia. Unpublished Masters dissertation. Available at:http://bdigital.cv.unipiaget.org:8080/jspui/bitstream/123456789/ 187/1/Fabio%20Vieira.pdf [accessed 20 August 2011].

World Bank (2011) World Governance Indicators: Country data report for Cape Verde 1996–2010. Available at: http://info.worldbank.org/governance/wgi/pdf/c49.pdf [accessed April 2012].

World Fact Book (2010) Africa: Cape Verde Available at: https://www.cia.gov/library/ publications/the-world-factbook/geos/cv.html [accessed April 2012].

Interviews

Brito A (2012) Director General of Higher Education in Cape Verde. Interviewed on Cape Verde, 29 February, Praia.

Barros C (20012) Former vice-chancellor of UNI-CV. Former member of the installations committee of UNI-CV. Interviewed 28 February 2012.

Correia e Silva A (2012) Minister of Higher Education, Science and Innovation. Interviewed on Cape Verde, 2 March 2012, Praia.

Emanuel B (2012) Statistics and Planning Technician at the Ministry of Higher Education, Science and Innovation. Interviewed 27 February 2012.

CHAPTER

GUINEA-BISSAU

4

4.1 Country profile

The Republic of Guinea-Bissau is a country situated in west Africa, bordered by Senegal to the north, Guinea-Conakry to the south-east and the Atlantic Ocean to the west. With a surface area of about 36 125 square km, it is one of the smallest PALOP in Africa, alongside São Tomé and Príncipe. Guinea-Bissau was the first PALOP country to become independent from Portugal. After 11 years of struggle for independence, the African Party for the Independence of Guinea and Cape Verde (PAIGC) unilaterally declared independence on 24 September 1973, which was later acknowledged by Portugal on 10 September 1974. Luís Cabral became the first president of independent Guinea-Bissau, as his brother, Amílcar Cabral, was shot dead in January 1973.

Luís Cabral governed the country until 1980, the year in which João Bernardo Nino Vieira, alleging deterioration of the country's economic conditions, deposed the Cabral's government in a bloodless *coup d'état*. After suspending the constitution, Vieira chaired a nine-member military Council of Revolution until 1984, the year in which a new constitution was approved, returning the country to civil government. From 1984 to 1999 Vieira ruled as president of the country. In the beginning of the 1990s, like many African countries, Guinea-Bissau abandoned the one-party political system and the socialist economic approach, and moved towards multiparty democracy.

In 1994, the first democratic elections were held, won by Vieira and PAIGC. In 1998, before the end Vieira's term in 1999, disagreements between Vieira and a military chief, Ansumane Mané, led to a civil war, opposing government forces and rebels loyal to Mané. The civil war forced Vieira to quit the presidency and to move to exile in Portugal. Elections held in 2000 led the opposition leader, Kumba Yalá, to power, but he was deposed by a military *coup d'état* in 2003. The elections held in 2005 enabled Vieira to resume power, but contradictions with General Batista Tagme Na Wai resulted in him being brutally murdered in 2009.

Malaim Bacai Sanhá was elected president in 2009, but military interventions intended to control the civil government continued, as in 2010, the current Guinean prime minister Carlos Gomes Junior was taken hostage by military chiefs. In 2011, Sanhá became terminally ill, leaving the country under the leadership of Carlos Gomes Junior while he went to France for treatment. Sanhá died in Paris, and new elections were called for in March 2012, with Gomes running for the top position with other fellow party members from the PAIGC as well as the opposition leader and former president, Kumba Yalá.

Guinea-Bissau has therefore experienced its share of political instability and a troubled historic trajectory, characterised by *coups d'état* and military interference in civilian governments. By April 2012, which is the time of finishing this report, Bissau was still in political turmoil. The *coup d'état* of 12 April 2012, which took place between the two rounds of the presidential election, plunged the country into serious mayhem. President Malam Bacai Sanhá died on 9 January 2012 and Raimundo Pereira, the speaker of the parliament, was due to act as head of state until elections were organised. But former prime minister and presidential candidate Carlos Gomez Junior, who was the favourite following the first round of voting, had said he planned to reform the armed forces. To anticipate and prevent the announced reform, a military junta seized power and halted the election. If the economic and financial sanctions envisaged by the Economic Community of West African States (ECOWAS) are implemented, they will have a substantial effect on the country's economy.

Constitutionally, the country is a semi-presidential republic: the president is the head of the state and the prime minister the head of the government. According to the website of the ministry of economy, planning and regional integration (INE-Guinea-Bissau 2011) the country had a population of about 1 520 830 inhabitants in 2009. Although Portuguese is the official language of the country, the majority of Guineans speak Creole (*Kriol*) which is the *de facto lingua franca* of the country.

Bissau is the political, economic and cultural capital of the country. Guinea-Bissau is one of the poorest countries in the world. In 2010 its nominal and per capita GDP were USD 825 million and USD 508 respectively (IMF 2010). The population's life expectancy was 46 years and child mortality rate: 99.8/1 000 in 2011 (The *CIA World Factbook* 2011). According to the United Nations Development Programme Report (UNDP 2010) in terms of HDI, Guinea-Bissau was in 167th position in a list of 192 countries, and its literacy rate was 64.6% in 2009 (UNDP 2009). According to the *Inquérito Ligeiro para a Avaliação da Pobreza*[1] (República de Guiné Bissau 2011, INE/UNDP 2010), about 69.3% of Guineans were poor[2], and 33% of the total Guinean population was extremely poor.

4.2 Background and historical context of higher education

While it can be argued that Guinea-Bissau's higher education has evolved and transformed significantly since its inception in the 1970s, the ultimate effects of these changes on the

---

1   Poverty Assessment Inquiry.
2   The document considers *poor* to be those living on less than USD 2 a day, and *extremely poor* those living on less than USD 1 a day.

underlying character of the country's higher education have not led to the constitution of an integrated higher education system. Nonetheless, the emerging features of higher education in Guinea-Bissau shows that its governance structures, funding mechanisms, the organisation of its primary processes – teaching and learning, research and services – and the general political, economic, and social condition under which the HEIs are operating are geared towards establishing an integrated and coordinated field. In addition, change from a central state-planned economy and regulation of higher education to an increasing reliance on market-driven competition in steering higher education can be observed in Guinea-Bissau. It can be argued that these changes are a result of global trends in higher education, but can also be linked to internal transformation in Guinea-Bissau in the last 30 years.

Guinea-Bissau does not have a public university. There is an on-going process to establish Amílcar Cabral University as its first public university. Thus, this chapter discusses the governance of higher education in Guinea-Bissau at faculty level, since there was no university structure. In this sense, the structure of this chapter is different from others where the discussion was situated at systemic level.

4.2.1 The development of post-secondary education

Bolama was the first capital of Guinea-Bissau during the colonial period from the 1870s until the 1940s. It was in Bolama that the Portuguese established the first teacher training school in Guinea. According to the former minister of education, Delfim da Silva, Bolama was regarded as an ideal place to establish the first HEI in Guinea, since it is located in the outskirts of Bissau (Da Silva 2012, interview). However, no university was ever established in Bolama. The Portuguese colonialists only established universities in two of their five colonies in Africa: Angola and Mozambique (Langa 2006, Bervejwik 2005). According to Perkin (1997: 29) Portugal was less active in colonial education than Spain; for instance, the first Brazilian university at Rio de Janeiro was not founded until 1920, nearly a century after independence. Thus, this particular feature of Portuguese colonialism is reflected in the African Portuguese speaking countries' delay in establishing HEIs.

Access to education, and higher education in particular, would constitute a key demand of the Guinean nationalism; and staff training was to occupy a central place in the concerns of the national liberation movement. This continued as a central concern for the state of Guinea-Bissau as a legacy of the national liberation struggle and the thinking of its leader, Amílcar Cabral (Landim 2011, quoted in Monteiro *et al.* 2011).

In 1977 Guinea-Bissau began to sketch the architecture for its first HEI. The National School of Law was established in 1978 with the purpose of training staff for public administration and law, but also for teaching (Landim and Monteiro 2012, interview).

Soon thereafter, in 1979, the vanguard pedagogic detachment Tchico Té was established as a school for teacher training for secondary education. The concept and style of this institution was reminiscent of the Cuban influence in the early years of post-independence national reconstruction. The Cuban government was at the forefront of supporting most African countries that gained independence and adopted socialism. In the same years the National

School for Physical Education and Sport was established. The process of establishing an institute of higher education supported by the German Democratic Republic, was interrupted by the coup of 14 November 1980 (Silva 2011 quoted by Monteiro *et al.* 2011; Silva 2012, interview). In the early 1980s another attempt to establish HEIs led to the creation of a unit to train civil servants, called the Administrative Training Centre (CENFA). In 1984 a research institute in the field of social sciences was established, the Instituto Nacional de Estudos e Pesquisa (INEP), followed in 1985 by the Instituto Nacional de Educação (INDE) which developed from a failed project to establish a pedagogical institute. In 1986 the Faculty of Medicine was established, but it did not form part of a university structure. The School of Medicine was upgraded and gained the status of a faculty ten years after its establishment in 1976. These changes occurred simultaneously with the restructuring of technical and vocational education in the country.

Table 4:1 shows the names of the HEIs in Guinea-Bissau and the year they were established.

Table 4.1 Post-secondary education institutions in Guinea-Bissau

Institution	Year of creation	Tutelage
School of Medicine	1976	Ministry of Heath
School of Law	1979	Ministry of Education and Ministry of Justice
National School of Health (ENS)	1974	Ministry of Health
Higher Normal School Tchico Té	1991	Ministry of Education
National School of Physical Education and Sports (ENEFD)	1979	Ministry of Education
Normal School 17 de fevereiro	1979	Ministry of Education
National School Amílcar Cabral (ENAC)	1975	Ministry of Education
Centre for Administrative Training (CENFA)	1982	Ministry of Education

Source: Author's field work 2012

4.2.2   The birth of university education: Faculties of Medicine and Law

4.2.1   Faculty of Medicine

The School of Law and the School of Medicine evolved to become the first two academic faculties in the history of Guinea-Bissau's higher education. These establishments marked the beginning of *de facto* university training in the country. In 1985 the School of Medicine was upgraded to a Faculty of Medicine, but officially it was elevated to the new status on 23 October 1986, by Decree 31/986, published in the Supplement to the Official Gazette 4386. The Faculty of Medicine was made official by a government Public Act of 12 November 1986. From its inception, the Faculty of Medicine received technical support from Cuba in the areas of medical assistance and scientific and technical support. The first cohort of 34 students enrolled in the pre-medicine programme. Until 1993 more than 30 Cuban teachers taught different subjects in the Faculty of Medicine, ranging from mathematics, physics and chemistry to biology and Spanish.

In July 1998 the political situation changed radically in Guinea-Bissau, with the advent of military unrest that lasted for more than eleven months and affected all sectors of society, including the cooperation with Cuba. It was only after an agreement was signed in July 2001 that the Cuban mission of seven members returned to its activities in Bissau to work at the National Hospital.

This mission of technical staff returned to Cuba on 11 May 2003 on the basis that the minimum working conditions were not in place. On 9 May 2005 a new group of 45 Cubans reached Guinea-Bissau, including 30 employees and 15 medical students working as assistants who were studying in Cuba. On 25 February, the head of the Cuban mission visited Bissau to assess *in situ* the living and working conditions that his team experienced in Bissau. Following his assessment the Faculty of Medicine was reopened on 20 January 2006. The reopening of the Faculty of Medicine was marked by the establishment of the Lusophone University Amílcar Cabral which formed the basis for admission into the medical programme. The students admitted to attend pre-university training in the area of medical sciences would qualify after passing a final exam and obtained the marks required to undertake a medical degree (*Licenciatura*).

The Faculty of Medicine is endowed with special status and is basically run by Cuban doctors of different specialisations and an administrative structure, with the ministry of public health of Cuba appointing the dean. The Faculty had units scattered across six different locations called medical or health regions. The idea of medical regions does not coincide with that of territory and governmental division. There are six medical/health regions:

- Health region of the autonomous sector of Bissau with headquarters in Bissau, at the Simon Mendes national hospital;
- Health Region of Cacheu, with two locations: one in Bula and the other in Santos Domingos;
- Sanitary Oio region, based in Mansoa;
- Health region of Bafatá, based in Bafatá;
- Health region of Gabu, based in Gabu; and
- Health region of Biombo, based in Quinhamel.

Between 1986 and 2011 the Faculty of Medicine graduated 340 medical doctors who are distributed throughout the country.

4.2.2.2   The Law Faculty

The establishment of the Law Faculty was a slow process that went on for more than a decade. The faculty evolved from the Law School established in 1979. The Law School was set up to train public servants and officials early after independence and was meant to fill the vacancies in the state bureaucracy created by the departure of the Portuguese settlers. A process of selection was put in place to attract secondary school graduates and professionals experienced in the administration of justice who did not have formal training, to become the first students of the new faculty.

The Law School operated with the support of teachers from different countries who had good diplomatic cooperation with Guinea-Bissau. At some point, problems of coordination hindered the Law School, leading to its closure for a few years. However, the dire need for trained personnel in the legal professions turned out to be increasingly critical for Government and it was decided to establish the Faculty of Law of Bissau (Decree 34/90, 26 November and amended again by Decree 4A/2005, 18 July). Since 1990 the country therefore has had a second university institution as the product of cooperation between the Republic of Guinea-Bissau and Portugal. Under the cooperation with Portugal exchange agreements were signed that enabled students and staff mobility.

The Law Faculty was established as a public institution with managerial, financial and academic autonomy. The main programmes offered in the institution are law and public administration. The course length is five years plus one year of a *propaedeutic* (i.e. an introductory course) which is usually called year zero. The current fee is CFA 70 000 (USD 133), equal for all levels, which makes the faculty the cheapest in the sub-region.

Although Guinea-Bissau still does not have a fully-fledged public university, in 2010 the government approved a new law for higher education and scientific research that established the condition under which the sector will be regulated (Lei do Ensino Superior e da Investigação Científica 2010). The new law regulates some aspects of the governance of higher education in Guinea-Bissau. For instance, according to the new law, rectors are appointed and dismissed by the council of ministers, upon the proposal of the minister responsible.

4.3   Trends of expansion, diversification and differentiation

As in most PALOP countries, the 1990s witnessed an increase in private higher education in Guinea-Bissau. According to Da Silva (2012, interview) the end of the socialist experiment in Guinea-Bissau, at the same time as in most countries of Eastern Europe and previously socialist Africa, represented a shift in the political economy to embrace a market-like economy and representative democracy. Da Silva (2012) mentions some factors that, in his view, contributed to the rapid marketisation and commercialisation of higher education in Guinea-Bissau, namely:

- The end or decline in financial support from the former socialist countries (including Cuba) that continued to pursue a socialist ideology;
- The dramatic reduction of scholarships for Guineans to study in former socialist countries; and
- The demographic pressure and increase of graduates from secondary schools that increased the need to offer local opportunities in their own country.

Pressure from society and the limited resources from government to supply public higher education forced a rapid liberalisation of education and thus opened the space for private providers.

As mentioned earlier, apart from the two isolated faculties of Law and Medicine, which had the support of Portugal and Cuba, Guinea-Bissau still does not have a public university. In 1981, Mario Cabral, then minister of education and culture, made advances in this direction with a proposal to establish a regional University (RENs-3), covering the small countries from PALOP without university education, namely: Guinea-Bissau, Cape Verde, and São Tomé and Príncipe (Monteiro and Da Silva, 1993). However, following changes in the political atmosphere, namely the *coup d'état* that ousted Luis Cabral from the presidency of the republic and the abandonment of the project to unite Guinea-Bissau and Cape Verde as one political entity, the idea of a regional university faded away along with the demise of the socialist experiment.

4.3.1 Emergence of private higher education

While in most African countries public universities had a near monopoly for years after independence, countries like Guinea-Bissau, São Tomé and Príncipe, and Cape Verde were exceptions to that trend. The latter countries had no (public) university several years after obtaining their independence. However, the market-friendly reforms initiated under structural adjustment programmes, deregulation policies, and the financial crisis of the state created an encouraging environment for the emergence of private higher education in Africa (Varghese 2004). The first institutions with university status in these countries were a product of the legislative measures initiated in the 1990s to enable the provision of higher education through private providers. In 1991 the Government approved Decree 07/91 of 20 May and for the first time made space for private operators in Guinea-Bissau's education. In this context, by 1995 the private Portuguese University Lusíadas was in advanced talks with the former minister of education Paulo Silva with a view to commencing operations in Guinea-Bissau.

The process was interrupted by the fall of the government headed by Colonel Saturnino da Costa. Immediately after, there was another initiative in conjunction with the University of Massachusetts (UMASS), led by former Finance Minister Manecas Santos and Prof. Donald Macedo to recover the bulk of the proposals by Carlos Lopes (Monteiro 2011). In 1996, by Presidential Decree, an installation committee was appointed and established, headed by Peter Mendy, Director of the INEP. But there was a stalemate regarding the configuration of the university/polytechnic institute, and the political-military conflict on 7 June would disrupt the process again (Landim 2012, interview).

However, during this interim period, in an effort to resolve the conflict in Casamance[3], Andrew Lewin, then ambassador of France in Guinea-Conakry and Senegal, presented to the French, Senegalese and Guinean authorities a proposal to establish a regional University

---

3   The Casamance Conflict is a low-level civil war that has been waged between the Government of Senegal and the Movement of Democratic Forces of Casamance (MFDC) since 1982 over the question of independence for the Casamance region.

of Senegambia, encompassing Guinea-Bissau, the Gambia and Casamance (Monteiro 2011, Landin 2012, interview). His proposal had little echo in the diplomatic circles, visibly hampered by his strong political involvement in the problems of southern Senegal (Casamance).

Finally, in 1999, the Government of National Unity created the Lusophone University Amílcar Cabral, personally and strongly pushed by Francisco José Fadul, then prime minister, and Galdé Baldé the then minister of education of the transitional government. The Lusophone University was established out of a public-private initiative, but the honeymoon period was so short that the two parts fell apart and the government abandoned the project. This issue is covered in more detail later in this chapter.

4.3.2   The rise of a new higher education landscape

The late 1990s were a period of profound political change, which had grave consequences for politics and the educational landscape of Guinea-Bissau. This period was marked by the establishment of Amílcar Cabral University, in collaboration with the Lusophone University of Portugal, in 1999 and a year later, the establishment of the University Hills Boé by a group of businessmen and intellectuals.

The small privately-run university Hills of Boe opened its doors in Guinea-Bissau in September 2003 (IRIN 2003; Lundim 2012; Monteiro, L 2012, interviews). Currently the country has a somewhat diverse higher education landscape. Bissau has six HEIs, one of which is public and the remaining others private institutions.

In fact, they are five universities in operation, all private: Lusophone University of Bissau (the former Amílcar Cabral University); the University Colinas de Boé (UCB); the Jean Piaget Institute; the Catholic University and the University of the West Africa International Sup management, a school-oriented private polytechnic, which operates in the old school of Taborda. With the emergence of new HEIs offering tertiary level education in Guinea-Bissau, the country's HEI landscape became diverse and differentiated. The Lusophone University offers 13 undergraduate programmes, UCB offers 4, joining the law courses and teacher training that already existed, given by the Faculty of Law of Bissau and the Escola Normal Superior Tchico Té.

The education system in Guinea did not have Grade 12. The two existing universities introduced a propaedeutic[4] year (APES), through which they offered to new students who had completed Grade 11 additional training to consolidate their knowledge of languages, computers as well as specific training in selected areas and disciplines.

The proportion of women is not satisfactory. However, female representation varies by institution and programme. UCB presents a more balanced gender parity and equity in their student body. Interestingly, it is the teacher training school that observed one of the lowest female representation, contrary to the situation in Guinea-Conakry and in most countries, where teaching is a profession dominated by women (Monteiro, H 2011, interview).

---

4   Propaedeutics or propedeutics is a historical term for an introductory course into a discipline.

Table 4.2 Courses and programmes offered by higher education institutions

Institution	Courses and programmes	Male	Fem	% Fem	Total
University Colinas de Boé	Public Administration and Social Economy	148	70	32.1	218
	Accounting and management	36	23	39.0	59
	Media and Marketing	21	38	64.4	59
	APES	147	111	43.0	258
	Sub-total	352	242	40.7	594
University Amílcar Cabral (No longer operating)	Pedagogy and Educational Sciences	5	5	50.0	–
	Architecture	23	5	–	28
	Medicine	81	46	–	127
	Nursing	46	30	39.5	76
	Administration and Company Management	87	60	40.8	147
	Economics	163	48	22.7	211
	Human Resources Management	16	22	57.9	38
	Social Work	6	12	66.7	18
	Organisational Communication and Journalism	22	27	55.1	49
	Computer Engineering	27	4	12.9	31
	Computer Science	–	–	–	–
	Sociology	27	17	38.6	44
	Law	60	25	29.4	85
	Pre-University Course	733	390	–	–
	Sub-total	1 187	635	34.9	1 822
Escola Normal Superior Tchico Té	Teacher Training	714	119	14.3	833
Total		2 253	996	30.7	3 249

Source: Monteiro H 2005

4.4 Amílcar Cabral University: A dream deferred

The Council of Ministers created the Lusophone University Amílcar Cabral (ULAC) by Decree Law 6/99 of 6 December, published in Official Gazette No. 49. The ULAC was managed by a private foundation (FUNPEC – Foundation for Promotion of Education and Culture) made up of the Government of Guinea-Bissau and a private Portuguese university (Lusophone University). For technical reasons ULAC began to operate fully at the end of the academic year 2003/2004.

Currently, the ULAC does not operate due to a disagreement between the government and the institution representing Lusophone University. The government removed itself from the joint venture, but Lusophone University continued to offer programmes using

Government facilities and premises (Landin 2012, interview). The set of colleges and faculties that were supposed to integrate a comprehensive institution were split up to operate in a school system of non-integrated university. The month of November 2008 marked the end of the joint administration, and the Government of Guinea-Bissau declared the transfer of the administration to its total bilateral partner, Lusophone University of Portugal, thus giving rise to the Lusophone University of Guinea (ULG).

The following quotation, lifted from a newspaper, shows the short-lived dream of Amílcar Cabral University.

> *President Henrique Rosa has formally opened the first public university in Guinea-Bissau, nearly 30 years after the small West African country achieved independence from Portugal. The autonomously managed university, created by a government decree in 1999, will admit its first students for a year of pre-degree course studies in January. Until now, Guinea-Bissau relied on bursaries to send its students to foreign universities, especially to Portugal, Cuba and Eastern Europe. However, Professor Tcherno Djalo, the rector of the new Amílcar Cabral University, said at the opening ceremony on Thursday this policy had proved a failure. He noted that about 80% of all Guineans educated abroad had decided to remain there to work afterwards. They therefore failed to contribute to building this desperately poor nation of 1.3 million people. The Amílcar Cabral University, named after the founder of the PAIGC liberation movement that fought for Guinea-Bissau's independence, will offer degree courses in education, law, medicine, veterinary medicine, engineering, agronomy, economics, sociology, modern languages and journalism. Students will be required to pay fees of 15 000 CFA (USD 26) per month – the equivalent of Guinea-Bissau's minimum wage. (IRIN 2003)*

It began as a national dream: the creation of a public university. Since independence Guinea-Bissau was always interested in establishing new fully fledged university in the country. The project failed for two main reasons: the first has to do with a significant number of scholarships given to Guineans to study abroad during the first years of independence, especially from Eastern Europe and Cuba. The new country often did not have enough candidates for these grants. There was a greater supply of scholarship grants than demand for it. Because of this, the government was not encouraged to establish a university in the country given also the small size of its population. The second reason was the shortage of qualified staff. This situation delayed the project of creating a university for a long period.

However, following the fall of socialist regimes in Eastern Europe and the end of the Cold War, along with the decline in the number of scholarships available and the increase of secondary education leavers, the need to establish a national university became a paramount and irreversible priority. However, the steps taken to that end did not succeed since it created a university with a hybrid public-private management system which proved to be a failure (Landim 2012, Da Silva 2012, Moteiro, L 2012, interviews).

In November 2011 the ministry of education set up a committee for the reopening of

Amílcar Cabral University (UAC) as a public university. During my fieldwork in Guinea-Bissau, I had the chance to interview the president of the re-establishment committee of Amílcar Cabral University, Mr Rui Landim.

> *Hopefully this time we can restore the initial proposal for a public university worthy of the name. The Faculties of Law and Medicine, as well as other units that we deem relevant will join the Amílcar Cabral University, as part of its organisational units.* (Landim, 12 February 2012, interview)

4.5   The governance of higher education

The governance and coordination mechanisms of higher education vary from country to country. In Guinea-Bissau the body that coordinates and supervises the activities and quality of higher education is the directorate general of higher education, which is part of the organisational structures of the ministry of education. As a result of this study it was found that the situation of higher education in the country in terms of governance, management and state control has not been consistent due to, amongst other factors, the political instability which brings constant changes of the governance structures. In the last 20 years, Guinea-Bissau had more than 27 ministers of education.

There were no clear structures for governance of higher education in Guinea-Bissau. The only structure at the time we visited Bissau was the directorate general for higher education, within the ministry of education. In an interview held with the director general of higher education in February 2012, he stated that he was in the process of reorganising all the legislation and would be calling on institutions operating in the country to follow suit (Ribeiro 2012, interview). However, this was before the last *coup d'etát* in March 2012 in the aftermath of the presidential election to fulfil the vacancy opened by the death of Bacai Sanhá in January 2012.

4.5.1   An unregulated system? Quality assurance

The rise of universities in Guinea-Bissau predated the existence of a basic law to govern the establishment and functioning of HEIs. This legal vacuum led to a disruption in the opening of the universities which also greatly influenced the supervision of curricula and consequently the quality of higher education. Currently, this regulation breach has been mitigated by the promulgation of legislation dealing with the development, improvement and control over higher education in Guinea-Bissau. Some of these are:

- Higher education law;
- Law on the status of training for a career in teaching;
- Law on higher education and scientific research; and
- Basic law of the education system.

Political instability frequently derailed plans for the establishment of legislation to regulate the system. The overall situation of higher education governance and management in Guinea-Bissau is still developing. In places where there is some kind of legislation, the implementation structures are very fragile. The sector has no system for quality assurance, accreditation of courses or validation of diplomas. Present course offerings are largely inadequate in meeting the needs and priorities of the country. For instance, despite its being an agricultural country, it has no programmes associated with the agricultural sciences; in addition there are no courses of history or anthropology, both of which are essential for knowledge creation, preservation and intervention in the socio-cultural and economic life of the country.

There is a lack of research centres. The existing universities are concentrated in the capital. In terms of infrastructure, most HEIs in the country operate under conditions that are inimical to quality university education. The universities often lack libraries, laboratories, functional classrooms, and have poor lighting. Nonetheless, the sector is very attractive in that there is strong demand from mostly young students, and the cost of education is relatively accessible in terms of affordability. There is even an increasing interest from international institutions in opening new institutions. The challenge is that there is little capacity and availability of regulation and management from the side of the ministry of education.

The new higher education and scientific research law defines in its second chapter the prerequisites for the establishment, suspension and cancellation of courses and programmes, covering both the universities and other kinds of HEIs. An application for the creation of a new course must be presented to the ministry of education, by the authority empowered to do so in accordance with the statutes of each institution (LESIC, Article 20, paragraph 1). The authorisation for the establishment of courses, as well as the power to suspend and cancel higher education courses, is vested in the directorate general of higher education (LESIC, Article 20, paragraph 2). Among the requirements for creating a course, the act lists the staff composition of the faculty, presentation of a curriculum and facilities for the provision of the course.

4.5.2   Financing and access in higher education

Like many other African countries, Guinea-Bissau faces inadequate public financing. However, the share of private resources in higher education financing is expanding. In Guinea-Bissau the contribution from households accounts for more than 50% of national expenditure (state and households) on higher education. Overall, HEIs in Africa generate about 30% of their income, though this ranges from less than 5% in Madagascar and Zimbabwe to 56% in Uganda and 75% in Guinea-Bissau (World Bank 2010). According to the World Bank report Guinea-Bissau spends about 70% of its higher education budget to support its students. In 2007 and 2008, more than 80% of Guinea-Bissau students' scholarships were for study abroad. However, household financing of higher education is relatively low when compared to household investment in other levels of education (30% of national expenditure in primary education and more than 45% in lower secondary education). This situation is peculiar to Africa and contributes to inequality in the education system, with the introduction of selection based on family resources well before a student's entry into higher education. Different forms of cost sharing are being implemented in most African countries. As of 2009, at least 26 countries in Africa charge either tuition fees or other types of fees such as examination fees, registration fees, identity card fees, library fees, and management information system fees.

From the emergence of higher education to the current academic year (2012), there has not been an official standard and unique set of criteria to regulate access to higher education in Guinea-Bissau. In the absence of a law governing higher education, access rules were very different from institution to institution. A general rule was for a candidate to possess a certificate of attendance of Grade 11 or equivalent. The two oldest universities (UCB and UAC) set up a preparatory year that candidates must successfully attend prior to enrolling in their degree courses. In the Law School of Bissau (FDB), the entry was subject to *numerus clausus*. Candidates were selected by the results obtained in a competitive entry exam and admitted according to vacancies. The remaining establishments had no special requirements other than possession of Grade 11 certificate. Each private institution establishes its fee rates. These schools live entirely off these earnings. However, this same condition occurs in some public institutions, namely the Faculty of Law of Bissau and CENFA.

4.6 ICT in higher education

ICT infrastructure in Guinea-Bissau can be characterised as inadequate and poor. A survey report compiled by Agyeman (2007) shows that there is little that can be said about enabling factors in ICT development in the country. For Agyeman (2007) assistance from donors and banks is required to help re-launch the country's economy and provide the infrastructure necessary to contribute to the deployment of ICTs.

The situation observed in 2007 remains practically the same in 2012, and the following are some of the impediments to the meaningful introduction of ICT into the curriculum at all educational levels in Guinea-Bissau:

- Government's limited and inadequate budgetary and financial resources
- Lack of high level information technology training institutes or schools
- General lack of ICT skills in the teaching population
- Low levels of teacher training
- Poorly equipped training institutions
- Irregular and insufficient electrical power supply across the country that obliges individuals to resort to fuel-powered generators at great cost – a cost that cannot be borne by the national government in the educational sector even when computers are made freely available by donors
- Inadequate and unavailable telecommunication infrastructure and services including the internet

- Concentration of national efforts on the massive reconstruction and rehabilitation of infrastructure destroyed in the 1998–1999 civil war

Adding to this dismal scenario, the political instability remains the greatest hindering factor to the development of the ICT infrastructure in the country. Just to illustrate this point, it is worth noting that the writing of this report was negatively affected by the most recent *coup d'état* in April 2012, since I could not correspond with my research assistant when most of the communication channels were shut down, including the internet.

REFERENCES

Agyeman OT (2007) *ICT in Education in Guinea-Bissau*. Available at: http://ddp-ext. worldbank.org/EdStats/GNBpro07.pdf [accessed April 2012].

Allafrica (2012) Guinea-Bissau: Chronology of Instability. Available at: http://allafrica.com/ stories/201204240908.html [accessed 23 April 2012].

CIA (2011) on Guinea-Bissau (2011) *The CIA World Factbook on Guinea-Bissau*. Available at: https://www.cia.gov/library/publications/the-world-factbook/geos/gv.html [accessed 22 August 2011].

INE-Guine-Bissau Instituto Nacional de Estatísticas da Guiné-Bissau. Available at: http:// www.stat-guinebissau.com/pais/index_quadro_fisico.htm [accessed August 2011].

International Monetary Fund (2010) Available at: http://www.imf.org [accessed 23 August 2011].

IRIN (14 November 2003) Guinea-Bissau: Government opens first university. Available at: http://www.irinnews.org/Report/47256/GUINEA-BISSAU-Government-opens-first-university [accessed April 2012].

Lei do Ensino Superior e da Investigação Científica (2010) *Ministério da Educação Nacional, Cultura, Ciência, Juventude e dos Desportos*. República da Guiné Bissau.

Monteiro H, Monteiro L and Cobna N (2011) O *Ensino Superior na Guiné-Bissau – Historial de um parto Difícil*. Available at: http://oraposaguineense.blogspot.com/2011/07/o-ensino-superior-na-guine-bissau.html [accessed September 2011].

Monteiro JH and Da Silva (1993) Exame longitudinal do comportamento dos indicadores do sistema educativo durante o PAE Bissau. In F Imbali *Os efeitos sócio-económicos do Programmea de Ajustamento Estrutural, na Guiné-Bissau* pp. 164–227) Bissau: Kacu Martel INEP.

República de Guiné Bissau (2011) *Ministério da Economia, do Plano e Integração Regional: Resultados definitivos*. Available at: http://www.stat-guinebissau.com/publicacao/ilap2.pdf [accessed 23 August 2011].

UNDP (2009) Retrieved from: http://hdr.undp.org/en/media/HDR_2009_EN_Complete. pdf, (Table H) [accessed 23 August 2011].

UNDP (2010) Retrieved from: http://hdr.undp.org/en/media/Lets-Talk-HD-HDI_2010.pdf [accessed 23 August 2011].

Varghese NV (2004) *Private Higher Education in Africa*. Available at: http://www.adeanet. org/pubadea/publications/pdf/adea_06_priv_higher_en.pdf [acccessed April 2012].

World Bank (2010) *Financing Higher Education in Africa*. Washington DC: The World Bank.

Interviews

Name	Position category	Institution	Date	Local
Alex Pierre	Director	Instituto Superior Politécnico Binhobló	29/03/2012	Instituto Superior Politécnico Binhobló
Alcides Gomes	Sub-Director	FDB	07/03/2012	FDB
Alfredo Gomes	Ex-Ministro da Educação	Ministério da Educação	16/02/2012	Ministério da Educação
Emiliano Gomes	Director	UCAO/Bissau		CIFAP
Fafali Kuodawo	Reitor	UCB		Colinas de Boé
Fernando Delfim da Silva	Ex-Ministro	Ministério da Educação	17/02/2012	Liceu João XXIII
Jailson Cuino	Ex-Director	Ensino Superior	16/02/2012	Hotel Malaica
João Ribeiro	Director	Ensino Superior	16/02/2012	Hotel Malaica
Lucy Monteiro	Assistente de programmea	UNESCO	16/02/2012	Hotel Malaica
Luís Alberto Taborda	Director	Sup Management		Escola de Condução Taborda
Mamadu Saliu Jassi	Ex-Director	Ensino Superior	16/02/2012	Ministério da Educação
Rui Landim	Presidente	Committee for the re-installation of University Amílcar Cabral	16/02/2012	Hotel Malaica

CHAPTER

5

MOZAMBIQUE

5.1 Country profile

The Republic of Mozambique is situated in the south-eastern part of Africa. It shares borders with South Africa and Swaziland to the south-west, with Zimbabwe to the west, Zambia and Malawi to the north-west, Tanzania to the north, and the Indian Ocean to the east. With a surface are of around 801 590 square km, Mozambique is the second largest Lusophone country in Africa. According to the latest census, carried out in 2007, the country had the following socio-demographic features: population: 20 579 265 inhabitants; life expectancy: 49.4 years; literacy rate: 50.4% (INE-MOZ 2012). According to IMF's World Economic Outlook Database, in 2011, the country's total nominal GDP was about USD 12 827 million and its nominal GDP per capita USD 582 (IMF 2012). The latest HDI report classifies Mozambique as one of the poorest countries in world: it ranks 184th of 187 countries, with an HDI of 0.322 (UNDP 2011).

Portuguese is the official language of the country, but the majority of Mozambicans speak Bantu languages. Mozambique is divided into 11 provinces and 129 districts, and Maputo is the capital city of the country, as well as its political and economic centre. Mozambique is a presidential republic. The president is both the head of the state and the head of the government. The president and the assembly are democratically elected by the popular ballot every five years.

Mozambique became independent from Portugal in 1975. The first independent government was ruled by Frelimo, a former nationalist movement which led the armed struggle for independence. Frelimo became a political party in 1977 and has been ruling the country since independence. From 1977 to 1985 the government of Mozambique experimented with socialism as a political and economic model of development and social construction.

However, international and internal factors forced a shift in policy, in the mid-1980s, from socialism to market-oriented policies. Internationally, the end of the Cold War in the late 1980s was the trigger for the government's decision to abandon socialism. Internally, the

16-year civil war, which was one of the consequences of the Cold War, forced the government to review its socialist policies. In the mid-1980s, the government joined the IMF and World Bank and began, from 1987 onwards, to implement structural adjustment programmes and to reform its political system. Since then Mozambique has adopted market-oriented policies and has changed the constitution to establish multi-party democracy.

As a consequence of civil war, Mozambique was in a desperate socio-economic situation by the late 1980s. Following the signing of the peace agreements in 1992, efforts have been made to rebuild the country and the economy. From the early 1990s to 2011, peace has been maintained and the annual average rate of economic growth has been around 7%, despite prevailing risks due to high rates of poverty (according to 2007 census, nearly half of Mozambicans live below the poverty line).

The country's future economic outlook continues to be positive, in particular as significant reserves of mineral resources, such as coal and natural gas, are being discovered and are attracting foreign investment.

5.2 The genesis of higher education

The development and current state of the field of higher education in Mozambique can be traced in three periods: (i) the colonial period, (ii) the socialist period, and (iii) the multi-party democracy and free-market period.

5.2.1 Colonial period

The colonial phase covers the period from 1962 to 1975. Unlike other European colonial powers, especially United Kingdom and France, which established HEIs in the beginning of the 20th century, and in particular during the immediate decades after the Second World War, Portugal did not establish any HEIs in its former colonies before the 1960s. Responding to pressures from both the international community and local Portuguese settlers, the Portuguese government created, through Decree law 44 530 of 21 August 1962, the first HEIs in Mozambique and Angola, named General University Studies.

The General University Studies of Mozambique (EGUM) was therefore the first HEI to be set up in Mozambique. To start with, EGUM offered academic programmes in education, medicine, agronomy, veterinary sciences and civil, mining, electrical and chemical engineering. By 1968, EGUM became Lourenço Marques University and extended its academic programmes to include applied mathematics, physics, chemistry, biology, geology, as well as Roman philology, history, geography, economics and metallurgical engineering (Mário et al. 2003, Berverwjik 2005, Langa 2006, Langa 2009). Although towards the end of Portuguese colonialism, in the late 1960s and the early 1970s, the Portuguese colonial government attempted to spread the idea that it was no longer racist, access to EGUM continued to be determined by colonial and racist ideology. By independence in 1975, only 40 black Mozambican students, representing less than 2% of the overall number of students, had entered Lourenço Marques University (Mário et al. 2003).

5.2.2   Independence and socialist period

The second phase of the development of higher education in Mozambique covers the period from 1975 to 1986. This phase is marked by the experiment of the socialist regime, which followed the country's independence in 1975. In 1976, following the wave of political changes brought about by independence, Lourenço Marques University was renamed after Frelimo's hero, and thus became Eduardo Mondlane University (UEM). During the early years of independence, in the late 1970s and early 1980s, UEM went through a difficult time. The number of students fell from 2 433 in 1975 to 750 in 1978. The teaching staff also decreased due to a massive exodus of Portuguese qualified personnel after independence. In 1978 there were only 10 Mozambican teaching staff. This shortage was filled by scientists and sympathisers from the socialist countries and/or the Soviet bloc, with which the Frelimo regime had strong relations (Mário *et al.* 2003).

The newly independent government not only changed the university's name to UEM, it also transformed its mission and academic programmes. In 1983, Law 4/83 was approved by the People's Assembly. Law 4/83 was the first law to institutionalise the Mozambican national system of education. Higher education was one of the sectors regulated by this law; others were primary, secondary and technical and vocational education. All sectors of education, including higher education, were controlled centrally by the ministry of education (MINED).

Law 4/83 determined that the mission of the whole educational system was to train a 'New Man', the builder of the socialist society. The university was specifically given the role of training cadres who would implement the government's socialist programme. In order to allow the university to fulfil this mission, MINED prescribed centrally all issues concerning higher education, such as curriculum, staff, students and the entire infrastructure (Beverwjik 2005:15). Thus issues concerning the micro-management of the institutions such as the number of students to enrol in higher education and the kind of courses to be undertaken were decided centrally by MINED (Law 8/79 of 3 July 1979, Mário *et al.* 2003, Gonçalves 2007).

Access to university did not require entrance examinations, and university attendance was free. The courses considered of lesser priority were closed, such as biology, chemistry, physics, geology, mathematics, geography, modern languages and educational sciences (Mário *et al.* 2003). Concerns like autonomy and academic freedom were simply overlooked during the socialist period. One of the sectors in which UEM participated actively was in the training of teachers for secondary schools to expand the education system, as illustrated by the creation of the Faculty of Education in 1980. In addition to this, other faculties were also created, such as the Faculty of Marxism-Leninism which had the mission of providing education to all students, and the Faculty for Combatants and Vanguard Workers, designed to enable party cadres to acquire higher education (Mário *et al.* 2003). Another way of allowing Mozambicans to have access to higher education was sending them abroad, in particular to socialist countries, such as East Germany, the Soviet Union, Czechoslovakia and Bulgaria.

Until 1984 UEM continued to be the sole HEI in the country. In 1985 and 1986 two new public HEIs came into existence: the Higher Pedagogical Institute (ISP) and the Higher Institute for International Relations (ISRI). ISP was designed to train teachers and was founded after the closure of UEM's Faculty of Education. Until the mid-1990s UEM, ISRI and ISP were the only HEIs in the country, and all of them were public.

5.2.3   Multi-party democracy and free-market period

The multi-party democracy and free-market phase covers the period from 1986 to date. During this period, the country experienced a transition from socialism to multi-party democracy and market-driven economy, with implications for higher education. The transition process was initiated in the mid-1980s and ended with the adoption of a new constitution in 1990, which formalised the shift from a one-party political system to a multi-party democracy, as well as from socialism to market-orientated economic policies. The democratic transition also resulted in the end of the civil war in 1992 that had started soon after independence between the government led by Frelimo and the rebel movement Renamo (Mozambican National Resistance). This fundamental socio-political and economic re-orientation had significant implications for the Mozambican higher education system.

The most important change for the higher education system was the introduction of a new law, 1/93, revised in 2003 (Mário *et al.* 2003:10, Beverwijk 2005: 15, Langa 2006: 18). This law marked the beginning of a 'new era' of multiple suppliers of higher education, including the opportunity for private institutions to participate in the provision of higher education. The new law also introduced the principles of 'autonomy' and 'academic freedom' to guide the functioning of HEIs, as quoted below:

> *Autonomy is the capacity of higher education institutions to exercise their powers, perform the necessary obligations, pursue academic freedom at an administrative, financial, patrimonial and scientific-pedagogic level, according to the institutions' objectives, strategies of the sector, policies and national plans. (*MESCT 2003*)*

As a result of the law, new private HEIs were created. The first private university to open was the Higher Polytechnic and University Institute (ISPU, later transformed into A-Polytechnic University), followed by the Catholic University (UCM). Both were established in 1995. ISPU and UCM were followed in 1998 by the Higher Institute of Science and Technology of Mozambique (ISCTEM), and by the Islamic Mussa Bin Bique University (UMBB). In 2000, the Higher Institute of Transport and Communication (ISUTC) was also established. From 2000 onwards private organisations, in particular businesses and religious organisations, continued to actively participate in the creation of private HEIs. By 2010 there were about 21 private HEIs (Taimo 2010, DICES 2009).

Alongside the founding of private HEIs, from the late 1990s onwards the government made efforts to expand the public sector of higher education. From 1999 to 2008, 14 new public HEIs were established, increasing the overall number of public HEIs from 3 to 17. As the following section shows in further detail, a quick glance at the names of the newly founded public HEIs reveals that the government policy trend was to create professional and polytechnic higher institutes and/or schools, rather than traditional universities. Only

2 of the 14 newly established public HEIs are labelled 'universities', the other 12 being either higher institutes or higher schools, and each of them is designed to train professionals in a specific and precisely defined professional area.

At present there are at least 38 different HEIs operating in Mozambique, but the accurate number may be nearly or slightly over 42, as new HEIs are founded every year, especially by private providers. Therefore, recent developments in the Mozambican higher education system display a process of expansion, differentiation and diversification (public vs. private; for-profit vs. non-profit; religious vs. secular).

5.3 Trends of expansion, diversification and differentiation

5.3.1 Expansion of higher education institutions

As referred to above, from the colonial period up to the mid-1980s, Mozambique had only one HEIs, the Eduardo Mondlane University. In the mid-1980s, two new public HEIs were created: the Higher Pedagogical Institute, created in 1985, which in 1995 became the Pedagogic University (UP); and the Higher Institute for International Relations (ISRI founded in 1986. In 1994 the UEM, the UP and the ISRI were the sole HEIs in the country.

From 1995 onwards, the number of HEIs expanded at a rapid rate. Apart from the macro-political and economic context of peace, stability, democracy and economic growth, three factors were responsible for the rapid increase in HEIs.

Firstly, there was a shortage of qualified personnel, scarce opportunity to attend higher education contrasting with a high demand for personnel holding a university degree, which resulted in a high demand for higher education in Mozambique. Regarding the high demand for personnel holding a university degree, Mário et al. (2003: 50) note that in the 1990s, students in high demand fields such as economics, management, law and engineering could secure employment even before completing their courses.

Concerning the scarcity of opportunities to attend higher education, Mário et al. (2003: 20) point out that in the late 1990s, only 0.16% of the age cohort 20–25, or 40 in every 100 000 inhabitants, studied at a HEI. With regard to the high demand for higher education, Mário et al. (2003: 18), quoting the Strategic Plan for Higher Education (2000), mention that in 1999 there were 10 974 applicants for 2 342 places available at UEM. But Mário et al. (2003: 19) also provide ratios illustrating that in the late 1990s, the excess of demand over supply characterised nearly all government institutions: at UEM, the ratio was 8:1; at ISRI 9:1; at UP 9:4, and at the newly founded Academy of Police Sciences (ACIPOL) it was 3:1. The high demand for higher education stimulated different stakeholders, both governmental and non-governmental, to create new HEIs. It also led the government to introduce competitive entrance examinations in 1991 as a means of selecting students to attend public HEIs (Dias 1992).

The second factor which was responsible for the expansion of HEIswas the approval of Law 1/93. As mentioned above, this law created the legal conditions for the establishment of non-governmental HEIs. As a result, a range of non-governmental organisations began to create HEIs. Two kinds of non-governmental groups were particularly active in the foundation of HEIs. One kind of group was religious communities, mainly Islamic and Christian-based denominations. The other kind of group was business companies or corporations.

By 2010, nearly all 21 non-governmental HEIs belonged either to religious entities or corporations. But very recently, other stakeholders, such as political parties, have also entered the market of higher education. For example, in 2011, Frelimo created a university named Nachingweia University (UNA).

The third factor that accounted for the expansion of HEIs was the government's willingness and intervention in the sector. Government intervention was driven not only towards enabling non-government organisations to participate in the provision of higher education, but also towards the extension of the public sector, through the creation of more public HEIs. As mentioned above, in 1994 there were only three public HEIs. Between 1999 and 2008, 14 new public HEIs came into existence. Most of the newly founded public HEIs were higher institutes or higher schools, specialised in a specific professional or technical area, rather than traditional universities. By 2010, the overall number of public HEIs was 17.

Due to these factors, the number of HEIs increased from 3 in 1994 to 38 by 2011. The 38 HEIs were the ones operating effectively by 2011. But as Tables 5.1 and 5.2 illustrate, the overall number of HEIs in existence is almost 42, since 4 more institutions were legalised in 2011.

5.3.2   Classification and differentiation of higher education institutions

According to Law 1/93, and its revised versions, Law 5/2003 and Law 27/2009, three criteria can be used to classify HEIs in Mozambique.

The first criterion is the type of property and mechanism of funding. According to this criterion, HEIs can be private or public. Public institutions are those owned by the state and depend on public funding, while private institutions are those owned by private collective entities, whether limited liability companies, foundations, Ptys or corporations, and whose main sources of income are private (Law 1/93, Article 9; Law 5/2003, Article 12; Law 27/2009, Article 13). Tables 5.1 and 5.2 below have been divided according to the nature of the ownership of the HEIs.

The second criterion is the focus and importance each higher education institution attributes to technical/professional training, scientific research and extension, and the kind of diploma/degrees that each higher education can award. Based on this criterion, HEIs may be universities, higher institutes, higher schools, polytechnic institutes, academies and faculties. Universities, higher institutes and faculties combine technical training with scientific research, while the mission of higher schools and polytechnic higher institutes is primarily technical/professional training. Regarding the ability to award degrees, polytechnic higher institutes are not allowed to award the PhD degrees (Law 5/2003, Article 13; Law 27/2009, Article 14). This second criterion is applicable both to public and to private HEIs.

Table 5.1 Public higher education institutions in 2011

Higher education institution	Date of creation and location of headquarters (main campus)	Campuses or branches in provinces
Eduardo Mondlane University (UEM)	1962, Maputo	Gaza, Inhambane, Quelimane
Pedagogical University (UP)	1985, Maputo	Maputo and nearly all 11 provinces
Higher Institute of International Relations (ISRI)	1986, Maputo	–
Academy of Police Sciences (ACIPOL)	1999, Maputo	–
Higher Institute of Health Sciences (ISCISA)	2003, Maputo	–
Military Academy (AM)	2003, Nampula	–
Higher School of Naval Sciences (ESCN)	2004, Maputo	–
Higher Institute of Accounting and Auditing (ISCAM)	2005, Maputo	–
Higher Polytechnic Institute of Gaza (ISPG)	2005, Gaza	–
Higher Polytechnic Institute of Manica (ISPM)	2005, Manica	–
Higher Polytechnic Institute of Tete (ISPT)	2005, Tete	–
Higher Institute of Public Administration (ISAP)	2005, Maputo	–
UNI-Lúrio University (UNI-Lúrio)	2006, Nampula	Niassa
Zambeze University (UNI-Zambeze)	2006, Sofala	–
Higher Institute of Journalism (ESJ)	2006, Maputo	–
Higher Institute of Arts and Crafts (ISAC)	2008, Maputo	–
Higher Polytechnic Institute of Songo (ISPS)	2008, Songo-Tete	–

Source: DICES 2009, Taimo 2010

Table 5.2 Private higher education institutions in 2011

Higher education institution	Date of creation and location of headquarters (main campus)	Campuses or branches in provinces
Higher Polytechnic Institute or A-Polytechnic University (ISPU or A-Polytechnic)	1995, Maputo	Quelimane, Tete
Catholic University (UCM)	1995, Beira	Nampula, Cuamba
Higher Institute of Science and Technology	1996	Maputo
Mussa Bin Bik University (UMBB)	1998, Nampula	Inhambane
Higher Institute of Transports and Communication (ISUTC)	1999, Maputo	–
Technical University of Mozambique (UDM)	2002, Maputo	Gaza
Saint-Thomas University of Mozambique (USTM)	2004, Maputo	–
Jean-Piaget University of Mozambique (UJPM)	200, Beira	–
Higher School of Economics and Management (ESEG)	200, Maputo	Manica, Tete
Higher Institute of Education and Technology (ISET)	200, Maputo	–
Christian Higher Institute (ISC)	2005, Tete	–
Higher Institute of Training, Research and Science (ISFIC)	2005, Maputo	–
Dom Bosco Higher Institute (Dom Bosco)	200, Maputo	–
Higher Institute of Technology and Management (ISTEG)	2008, Maputo	–
Monitor Higher Institute (ISM)	2008, Maputo	Distance learning
Higher Institution of Communication and Image (ISCIM)	2008, Maputo	–
Indian University of Mozambique	2008, Maputo	–
Maria Mother of Africa Higher Institute	2008, Maputo	–
Higher Institute of Management, Finance and Business (ISGCOF)	2009, Maputo	–
Alberto Chipande Higher Institute of Technology (ISTAC)	2009, Beira	–
Higher Institute of Science and Management (INSCIG)	2009, Nacala-Nampula	–
Adventist University of Mozambique	2011, Beira	–
Frelimo or Nachingweia University	2011, Maputo	–
Higher Institute of Management and Business of Manjacaze	2011, Gaza	–

Source: DICES 2009, Taimo 2010

The third legal criterion used to classify HEIs, in particular private ones, is *profitability* (Law 27/2009, Article 13). Some private HEIs are supposed to be, at least theoretically, for-profit institutions while others are non-profit. However, the law doesn't provide measures that enable one to determine whether a specific institution is for-profit or not. More likely, the profitability is linked to the nature of the founding entity, whether this is a (philanthropic) association/organisation or a business corporation. However, based on the fees paid in the majority of private HEIs, it can be argued that all of them are for-profit: in both those owned by religious organisations and in those owned by corporations, monthly fees range from

USD 100 to USD 300. Some degree of profitability is also present in public HEIs, where evening academic programmes cost almost the same as in private HEIs.

Based on these criteria, and as Tables 5.1 and 5.2 illustrate, the majority of Mozambican HEIs are private. Moreover, both government and non-government bodies have, since the mid-1990s, invested more in creating higher institutes or higher schools than in establishing traditional universities. The government was active in creating HEIs, but most of them were specific to a particular professional domain. For example, the Academy of Police Sciences specialises in training high police officials; the Military Academy in training high-ranking army officials; the higher polytechnic institutes specialise in training professionals for specific economic sectors, such as agriculture and mining. Regarding non-governmental stakeholders, two groups were particularly active in founding HEIs: religious denominations, in particular Christian and Islamic communities, and business corporations.

5.3.3 Academic programmes offered in different higher education institutions

The various HEIs offer different academic programmes, ranging from arts, humanities, social sciences, business sciences (i.e. soft sciences), to natural sciences, applied sciences and engineering (i.e. hard sciences). Some are multifunctional, which means that they offer nearly all areas of academic, cultural and professional training, like UEM. Others are limited to a specific academic and professional area, like ISCISA (health), ACIPOL (police), AM (army), ESEG (business). Tables 5.3 and 5.4 below show the scientific-professional areas covered by each HEI in Mozambique.

Table 5.3 Academic programmes offered by public higher education institutions

| Public higher education institutions | Academic programmes offered | | | | |
	Health	Arts, Social Sciences, Communication and Education	Engineering and Natural Sciences, Mathematics and Statistics	Law and Business Sciences	Civil Service, Defence and Security
Eduardo Mondlane University (UEM)	Medicine, Public Health	Literature, Linguistics, Philosophy, Language Teaching: Portuguese, French, English and Bantu languages	Mathematics, Statistics, Biology	Economics, Management, Finance, Accounting, Tourism, Law	Public Administration

Table 5.3 Academic programmes offered by public higher education institutions (cont.)

Public higher education institutions	Academic programmes offered				
	Health	Arts, Social Sciences, Communication and Education	Engineering and Natural Sciences, Mathematics and Statistics	Law and Business Sciences	Civil Service, Defence and Security
Eduardo Mondlane University (UEM)	None	Geography, Anthropology, Sociology, Political Sciences, Archaeology, Journalism, Information Sciences, Music and Theatre, Organisation and Management of Education, Environmental Education, Psychology, Child Education and Development, Adult Education, Higher Education, Curriculum Studies	Geology, Physics, Chemistry, Oceanography, Meteorology, Civil Engineering, Computer Science, Engineering, Electrical Engineering, Electronic Engineering, Agricultural, Engineering, Physical Engineering, Environmental Engineering, Forestry Engineering	None	None
Pedagogical University (UP)	Teaching of sports and physical education	Language Teaching: English, Portuguese, French Social Sciences Teaching: Geography, History, Philosophy Educational Sciences: Psychology, Pedagogy, Didactics, Educational Management	Natural and Exact Sciences Teaching: Biology, Chemistry, Mathematics, Physics, Statistics and Information Management	Economics, Management, Finance, Accounting	None
Higher Institute of International Relations (ISRI)	None	None	None	None	Public Administration, Diplomacy
Academy of Police Sciences (ACIPOL)	None	None	None	None	Police Sciences

Table 5.3 Academic programmes offered by public higher education institutions (cont.)

Public higher education institutions	Academic programmes offered				
	Health	Arts, Social Sciences, Communication and Education	Engineering and Natural Sciences, Mathematics and Statistics	Law and Business Sciences	Civil Service, Defence and Security
Military Academy (AM)	None	None	Military Engineering	None	Military Professions
Higher School of Naval Sciences (ESCN)	None	None	Electronic/ Telecommuni- cations Engineering, Engineering of Maritime Machines, Maritime Navigation Engineering	None	None
Higher Institute of Health Sciences (ISCISA)	Nursing, Biomedical- Laboratorial Technology, Surgery, Hospital Management and Administration, Occupational Therapy, Public Health	None	None	None	None
Higher Institute of Accounting and Auditing of Mozambique (ISCAM)	None	None	None	Accounting and Auditing Management	None
Higher Institute of Public Administration (ISAP)	None	None	None	None	Continuing Training of Civil Servants
Higher Institute of Arts and Crafts (ISAC)	None	Visual Arts, Cultural Animation	None	None	None
Higher Polytechnic Institute of Gaza (ISPG)	None	None	Agricultural Engineering, Zoology	None	None

Table 5.3 Academic programmes offered by public higher education institutions (cont.)

Public higher education institutions	Academic programmes offered				
	Health	Arts, Social Sciences, Communication and Education	Engineering and Natural Sciences, Mathematics and Statistics	Law and Business Sciences	Civil Service, Defence and Security
Higher Polytechnic Institute of Manica (ISPM)	None	None	Agricultural Engineering, Forestry Engineering, Zoology, Eco-tourism and Fauna	Accounting and Auditing Management	None
Higher Polytechnic Institute of Tete (ISPT)	None	None	Engineering of Mines	Accounting and Auditing	None
Higher Polytechnic Institute of Songo (ISPS)	None	None	Geology, Mechanical Engineering, Electronic Engineering, Civil Engineering	None	None
Higher School of Journalism (ESJ)	None	Journalism, Public Relations, Advertising/ Marketing	None	None	None
Zambeze University (UNI-Zambeze)	Medicine, Dental Medicine, Pharmacy	None	Civil Engineering, Procedures' Engineering, Mecatronic Engineering, Informatics Engineering, Agricultural Engineering, Rural Development Engineering, Natural Resources/ Environmental Engineering, Forestry Engineering	Management, Economics, Accounting and Finance, Law	None

Table 5.3 Academic programmes offered by public higher education institutions (cont.)

Public higher education institutions	Academic programmes offered				
	Health	Arts, Social Sciences, Communication and Education	Engineering and Natural Sciences, Mathematics and Statistics	Law and Business Sciences	Civil Service, Defence and Security
Lúrio University (UNI-Lúrio)	Medicine, Dental Medicine, Pharmacy, Nutrition, Optometry, Biology	None	Computer Science, Engineering, Architecture	None	None

Source: Author's field work, HEIs' websites and promotional materials

Table 5.4 Academic programmes offered by private education institutions

Public higher education institutions	Academic programmes offered			
	Health	Arts, Social Sciences, Communication and Education	Engineering and Natural Sciences, Mathematics and Statistics	Law and Business Sciences
Higher Institute of Technology and Science (ISCTEM)	Medicine, Dental Medicine, Pharmacy	Sociology	Computer Science, Engineering, Architecture and Urban planning	Business Communication, Business Management, Applied Management, Accounting and Finance, Law, Public Administration
Higher School of Economics and Management (ESEG)	None	None	Civil Engineering	Business Management, Tourism Management, Accounting and Financial, Law
Christian Higher School (ISC)	None	Theology, Psychology	None	None
Higher Institute of Technology and Management (ISTEG)	None	Communication Sciences, Social and Organisational Psychology	None	Economics, Business Management, Human Resources Management, Accounting and Finance Law

Table 5.4 Academic programmes offered by private education institutions (cont.)

Public higher education institutions	Academic programmes offered			
	Health	Arts, Social Sciences, Communication and Education	Engineering and Natural Sciences, Mathematics and Statistics	Law and Business Sciences
Higher Institute of Transport and Communication (ISUTC)	None	None	Mechanical and Transport Engineering, Informatics and Telecommunication Engineering, Civil Engineering	Management, Finance
Higher Institute of Communication and Image (ISCIMA)	None	None	None	MBA in partnership with the Technical University of Madrid
Maria Mother of Africa Higher Institute	None	Education, Social Services	None	None
Higher Institute of Management, Business and Finance (ISGCOF)	None	None	None	Management, Economics, Accounting and Auditing, Law
Dom Bosco Higher Institute (training of teachers for professional education)			Agricultural Teaching, Tourism Teaching	Administration Teaching, Accounting and Auditing teaching
Monitor Higher Institute (distance learning) (ISM)	None	Psychology, Sociology	Computer Science, Engineering, ICT/Computer Science	Accounting and Auditing, Financial Management, Human Resources Management, Economics Law
Alberto Chipande Higher Institute of Science and Technology (ISTAC)	Medicine, Health Sciences, Pharmacy, Public Health	Psychology, Sociology	None	Accounting and Auditing
Higher Institute of Science and Technology (ISET)	No data	No data	No data	No data
Higher Institute of Training, Research and Science (ISCFIC)	No data	No data	No data	No data

Table 5.4 Academic programmes offered by private education institutions (cont.)

Public higher education institutions	Academic programmes offered			
	Health	Arts, Social Sciences, Communication and Education	Engineering and Natural Sciences, Mathematics and Statistics	Law and Business Sciences
Higher Institute of Science and Management (INSCIG)	No data	No data	No data	No data
A-Polytechnic University (A-Polytechnic)	None	Communication Sciences, Educational sciences, Psychology, Sociology	Civil Engineering, Computer Science, Architecture and Design	Accounting and Auditing, Business Management, Finance and Management, Economics, Tourism Management, Law, Political Sciences
Catholic University (UCM)	Medicine, Nursing, Hospital Management and Administration, Clinical and Laboratory Analysis, HIV/AIDS, Public Health	Administration and Management of Education, Adult Education, Educational Sciences, Social Education, Anthropology, Social Service, Psychology, Communication Sciences	Computer Science/ICT, Civil Engineering, Food Engineering, Information Technology and System, Agricultural Engineering, Agribusiness, Plant Production, Engineering, Rural Develop-ment, Agriculture	Tourism Management, Development Management, Business Administration, Economics and Business, Management, Human Resources Management Marketing, Ports Management, Regional Planning, Law
Université Saint Thomas (USTM)	None	Sociology, Philosophy	ICT, Agricultural Sciences, Rural Development	Management, Accounting and Auditing, Economics, Management and Finance Law
Technical University of Mozambique (UDM)	None	None	Environmental Engineering	Business Management, Accounting and Auditing, Management and Finance, Human Resources Management, Law
Mussa Bin Bik University (UMBB)	None	None	None	Business Management, Accounting and Auditing, Law

Table 5.4 Academic programmes offered by private education institutions (cont.)

Public higher education institutions	Academic programmes offered			
	Health	Arts, Social Sciences, Communication and Education	Engineering and Natural Sciences, Mathematics and Statistics	Law and Business Sciences
Jean Piaget University (UJPM)	None	Sociology	Systems Engineering	Management, Economics Law
Indian University of Mozambique	No data	No data	No data	No data

Source: Author's field work, HEIs' websites and promotional materials

As Tables 5.3 and 5.4 above illustrate, UEM is the only public higher institution that covers nearly all areas of scientific, cultural and professional training, and it is the country's largest institution in terms of the scope of academic programmes it offers and the size of its infrastructure. UEM is followed by UP in terms of range of programmes offered and size of its infrastructure, though the majority of UP's academic programmes are oriented towards teacher training. Among the oldest institutions, ISRI is the smallest, both regarding the variety of its academic programmes and the size of its infrastructures. ISRI only offers two BA Honours degrees in public administration and in international relations. In 2011, it also introduced Masters degree programmes in development studies and policy analysis.

Concerning the newly created institutions, of the 32 institutions (excluding UEM, UP, ISRI), for which data is available, 4 offer academic programmes in the area of civil service, security and defence, 6 in the area of health, 12 in the area of social sciences, arts, education and communication, 16 in the field of engineering and 23 in the field of law and business sciences. The government has established 14 HEIs offering academic programmes in the fields of civil service, security and defence (ISAP, ACIPOL and AM), health (ISCISA, UNI-Zambeze, UNI-Lúrio), law and business sciences (ISCAM, UNI-Zambeze, ISPM, ISPT), communication and arts (ESJ, ISAC), and engineering and natural sciences (ESCN, ISPG, ISPM, ISPT, ISPS, UNI-Zambeze, UNI-Lúrio).

Engineering and the natural sciences are the fields in which the state has invested most. Since the late 1990s, the state has established five public higher polytechnic institutes and two new public universities, all of which offer academic degrees in engineering. Four of the five higher polytechnic institutes and the two newly created universities are located outside Maputo in the Central and Northern provinces.

The preference for locating new HEIs in these provinces represents an effort made by the government to reduce regional disparities and to relieve the southern part, in particular Maputo, of the pressure of satisfying the demand for higher education.

The state invested less in disciplines such as arts, social sciences, education and communication. The government did not found HEI for social sciences; it only founded one new institution specialised in arts and crafts, ISAC, and one to train journalists and communication professionals, ESJ. Nevertheless, the state invested significantly in this area of education, albeit not through the creation of new autonomous institutions, but through the establishment of new branches of Pedagogical University in provinces. Nearly all eleven provinces have at least one branch of UP, designed to train teachers in a wide range of academic disciplines.

Tables 5.3 and 5.4 above also show the scientific and professional domains covered by non-governmental organisations' investment in higher education. Private stakeholders established 23 HEIs between 1995 and 2011. Data on academic programmes offered was available for 18 of the 23 private HEIs. From the 18 institutions, 15 offer academic programmes in the fields of law and business sciences, 10 in the area of arts, social sciences, education and communication, 3 in the field of health, and one in the area of civil service. Law and business sciences were and continue to be the preferred area of private investment in higher education, followed by two areas, engineering and natural sciences, and arts, social sciences, education and communication.

The majority of academic programmes offered by public and private higher education providers issue a BA Honours degree. Since the early 2000s there is also an increase in Masters programmes, in particular in the fields of law, business sciences and arts, social sciences and education. But the number and variety of Masters programmes is limited, in comparison to BA Honours programmes. PhD degrees are very limited in Mozambique: in the public sector only UEM offers one PhD programme in Linguistics, while in the private sector, A-Polytechnic and ISCTEM offer a limited number of PhD programmes in partnership with Portuguese universities, and UCM offers a PhD programme in the field of education.

5.3.4 Expansion in student enrolment

The expansion in the number of HEIs was accompanied by an increase in student enrolment. In the mid-1990s, the number of university students was less than 4 000. By 1999, this number had increased to 12 000, and in 2002 it had risen to almost 20 000. The rapid increase from 1996 onwards was partly due to the opening of private HEIs, whose share of students rose from less than 300 in 1996 to almost 2 600 by 1999. But the increase in enrolment in governmental institutions was mostly responsible for the rapid increase in overall university student enrolment during the 1990s: from 1990 to 1999, enrolment in public institutions more than doubled, from 3 750 to 9 201 students (Mário *et al.* 2003, Langa 2006).

During the 2000s, the increase in enrolment became overwhelming. In 2006, the overall number of students' enrolled was 43 233; of these 11 311 students were enrolled in private institutions, and 31 922 in public institutions. In private institutions, A-Polytechnic, UCM, ISCTEM, USTM and UDM concentrated the greater share of enrolment: A-Polytechnic with 2 570 students, UCM with 2 223 students, ISCTEM with 1466 students, USTM with 1 173, and UDM with 1 108 students in 2006. Each of the other private institutions operating in 2006 had fewer than 1 000 students.

In the public sector, UEM and UP were particularly responsible for the growth in student enrolment. In 2005, UEM had 11 517 students and, in 2006, 14 199; UP had 5 539 students in 2005, and 15 039 in 2006. Each of the other public HEIs functioning in 2006 had fewer than 400 students, and some had even fewer than 100 students (DICES 2008).

From 2006 to 2010, the number of university students more than doubled again, from over 40 000 to more than 100 000 students. Again, the public sector was responsible to a great extent for the growth. Latest data indicates that in 2010, UP had nearly 40 000 students and UEM around 30 000 (DICES 2010). This growth is particularly due to the opening of evening fee-paying classes at UEM and UP. The other 30 000 students are enrolled either in small public HEIs or in private institutions.

Figure 5.1 Growth in number of students and graduation rates

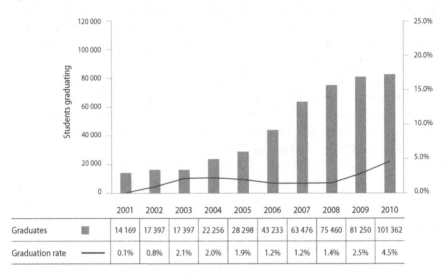

		2001	2002	2003	2004	2005	2006	2007	2008	2009	2010
Graduates	■	14 169	17 397	17 397	22 256	28 298	43 233	63 476	75 460	81 250	101 362
Graduation rate	——	0.1%	0.8%	2.1%	2.0%	1.9%	1.2%	1.2%	1.4%	2.5%	4.5%

Source: MINED 2012

5.3.5   Projected scenarios of growth in student enrolment 2012–2025

Table 5.2 shows that despite government policies to increase the gross participation in higher education, Mozambique still trails the African average of 6%. In its new strategic plan (2012–2020), government has set out to expand access as well as enhance quality. In analysing the development of effective student enrolments, government makes the following projections.

In the *first scenario,* although a growing number of students is projected from the current 101 362 to 132 533 in 2020 and 149 962 in 2025, representing an overall growth of 30.8% and 48.0%, respectively, the underlying assumption is that there will be no increase in the proportion of students in relation to the total population. Although this hypothesis seems convenient in terms of a gradual evolution and costs, it has the disadvantage of not considering the necessary development of the country in relation to regional levels, keeping the country relatively low from the perspective of human development.

Figure 5.2 Three scenarios of student enrolment and graduation rates 2012–2020

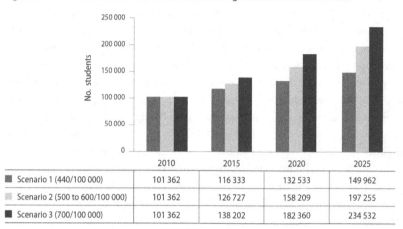

	2010	2015	2020	2025
■ Scenario 1 (440/100 000)	101 362	116 333	132 533	149 962
▨ Scenario 2 (500 to 600/100 000)	101 362	126 727	158 209	197 255
■ Scenario 3 (700/100 000)	101 362	138 202	182 360	234 532

Source: MINED 2012

The *second scenario* shows a slight recovery in relation to the countries of the region, assuming a gradual shift of 440 students per 100 000 to 500 students by 2017, followed by an increase to 600 students per 100,000 inhabitants by 2025, thus increasing the number of students from the current 101 362 to about 158 209 in 2020 and 197 255 in 2025. This corresponds to an overall growth of 56.1% and 95.0%, respectively. This scenario may be considered ideal, given the need to improve the current situation of higher education in Mozambique, particularly in terms of recruitment and training of academic staff and in terms of building new infrastructure.

The *third scenario*, which is a real challenge for the country, consists in the increase of the current ratio of 440 students per 100 000 inhabitants, to about 700, which is almost double the current situation. The number of students will increase from 101 362 to 182 360 by 2020, and to 234 532 by 2025, representing an overall growth of 80.0% and 131.4%, respectively. This scenario should be accompanied by an effective monitoring of resources and quality assurance and could effectively better respond to the current pace of development of secondary education. Moreover, it would mean not only an increase but also a correction of the level of funding for higher education relative to GDP, approaching about 1.0 to 1.2 by 2025. This hypothesis would require an increase of about 130 000 new student places in Mozambican higher education (MINED 2012).

5.4   Changes in higher education governance

Before the approval of Law 1/93, higher education in Mozambique was centrally controlled by the ministry of education. The principles of autonomy and academic freedom, stated in Law 1/93, significantly reduced MINED's interference in the sector. HEIs ceased to be dependent on the ministry in many respects, such as the courses they could offer and the careers to be chosen by students (Beverwijk 2005). The rectors' role in higher education policy making was increased, as they were appointed to the Higher Education Council (CES). CES brings together MINED and all HEIs at the highest level in a collaborative effort to shape the mechanisms that support policy implementation in the sector (Chilundo 2010).

The National Council on Higher Education (CNES) is a consultative board for the council of ministers and a broader forum with the mandate of overseeing the implementation of planning processes between the higher education sectors. CNES comprises members from various sections of government, CES, representatives from research and HEIs, business associations and civil society. CNES is responsible for advising the council of ministers on the approval of new institutions, for funding public HEIs, and for all sector policy decisions (Beverwijk 2005). As a sounding board for evaluating the progress of policy implementation, CNES functions as a vital body in scrutinising new policies and proposals before they were presented to the Council of Ministers for approval and legislation (Chilundo 2010).

In the mid-1990s, due to the challenges that the rapid expansion, diversification and differentiation of higher education had given rise to, such as coordination, quality assurance and supervision, regional and social equity, the government was called upon again to play a crucial role in the sector. There was a consensus that a governmental board should be created to coordinate the sector at national level. As a consequence, in 2000, the ministry of higher education, science and technology (MESCT) was established. MESCT's mission was to guide and support the expansion and diversification of higher education, as well as to put science and technology on the government's agenda.

Due to some degree of dissonance among different key stakeholders (rectors, council of rectors, MESCT) concerning their respective power and influence in the sector (Beverwijk 2005), the MESCT was disbanded in 2005 and higher education once again reverted to the ministry of education. A coordinating board, the National Directorate for Coordinating Higher Education (DICES), replaced MESCT. DICES is directly dependent on the ministry of education, as its national director is appointed by the minister of education.

The new government that took office in 2010 also made some significant changes. One minister and three deputy ministers of education have been appointed. One of the three deputy ministers of education is responsible for the portfolio of higher education. Currently, higher education issues are decided, coordinated and determined at national level by the ministry of education, the National Council for Higher Education, and the National Council for Assessing the Quality of Higher Education (CNAQ). CNAQ is an advisory board of the ministry of education for issues regarding quality assurance. The Council for Higher Education, made up of rectors is an advisory board of the council of ministers on all higher education issues.

At institutional level, each HEI is governed and coordinated by the rector, deans of academic units and the institutional collegiate boards, such as the University Council and the Academic Scientific Council. In this manner, the principles of autonomy and academic freedom are given effect in HEIs.

5.5   Financing higher education

Public and private HEIs are funded differently. Public institutions are funded from four different sources: government funding, donor support, student fees, and income generating activities. The government's budget is the public institutions' largest source of revenue. About 97% of public institutions' budget is supported by the government, and each institution negotiates its budget directly with the ministry of finance. Donor support takes different forms, including scholarships and training opportunities, technical assistance, research support and capacity building. Student fees are also another source of revenue for public institutions (Beverwijk 2005), but their amount is negligible: in 2009, fees at UEM and UP were around USD 100 per year (Johnstone and Marcucci 2010). The private institutions are funded from three sources: donor support, capital venture, and student fees, but student fees are their essential sources of revenue. Monthly fees at private institutions are around USD 150 to USD 300.

There is consensus, among different stakeholders, including the government and rectors, that the funding situation described above is problematic, mainly in view of the expansion and sustainability of public higher education, and its equity, efficiency and accountability. Currently, the government pays about USD 2 500 per year per student enrolled in public higher education. As referred to above, the government made a significant effort to expand higher education opportunities: the number of public HEIs rose from 3 in 1994 to 17 by 2011, and the number of students enrolled in public institutions increased from less than 4 000 in 1994 to nearly 100 000 by 2011.

However, the higher education participation rate in Mozambique is still low, with less than 1% of the typical age cohort students attending higher education, compared to the African average rate of 5%. Thus in order to keep on expanding higher education, the government either has to increase its financial share, or else maintain or even reduce the current USD 2 500 per student, which would have negative consequences on the quality of education offered. To keep on expanding higher education and sustain it, other actors, such as families and corporates, should participate or increase their financial participation in higher education, e.g. by means of a cost-sharing model (Teixeira et al. 2006).

The second challenge concerns equity. The on-going system of funding is considered to be socially unfair, since the government pays the same amount for everyone, irrespectively of their socio-economic position. With the current system of fees in public institutions, in which everyone pays the same fees no matter how rich and poor s/he is, the rich students are the ones who benefit most from the system, both because they are better prepared and because they save money they could use for paying fees. The government intends to change this situation, by introducing an approach in which those who can afford are invited to pay a share for their education, and families in need receive government support (Chilundo 2010).

The third challenge concerns accountability and efficiency. Each public HEI negotiates its budget with the ministry of finance according to its needs. There is no mechanism for making HEIs accountable for the money they receive. The government argues that a new approach of funding should be introduced, not only based on institutional necessities, but also on their respective performance.

The fourth challenge concerns the possibility of the government participating in the funding of private HEIs, through specific programmes and mechanisms. So far, private HEIs basically rely on student fees, and government support is insignificant or non-existent. In order to make the funding of higher education more sustainable, equitable, accountable and efficient, a new approach of higher education is being introduced, called the Strategy for the Funding of Higher Education (Chilundo 2010).

Table 5.5 Evolution of state budget for education (000 MT)

| Academic year | State budget | Budget | | Total | % Education in the budget | % HE in the education budget |
		General education	Higher education			
2005	40 321 861	6 663 709	1 185 677	7 849 386	19.5	15.1
2006	46 955 000	7 977 144	1 340 440	9 317 584	19.8	14.4
2007	65 819 000	11 645 211	1 539 055	13 184 266	20.0	11.7
2008	80 331 000	15 150 507	2 010 725	17 161 232	21.4	11.7
2009	90 401 000	16 377 501	2 562 935	18 940 436	21.0	13.5
2010	117 977 200	15 201 405	3 465 399	18 666 804	15.8	18.6

Source: General State Accounts (several years) and Budget Execution Report, fourth quarter 2009

Table 5.6 Evolution of budget and expenditure on higher education, 2005/2010 (000 MT)

| Academic year | Operation | Investment | | | Total | % operation | Expenditure on HE | % Expenditure on HE |
		Total	Internal	External				
2005	915 734	269 943	90 855	179 088	1 185 677	77.2	913 729	77.1
2006	980 121	360 319	95 053	265 266	1 340 440	73.1	1 104 209	82.4
2007	1 085 168	453 888	128 230	325 658	1 539 055	70.5	1 374 520	89.3
2008	1 363 645	647 080	303 976	343 104	2 010 725	67.8	1 945 931	96.8
2009	1 610 856	952 079	473 209	478 870	2 562 935	62.9	2 456 793	95.9
2010	2 467 156	998 243	874 759	123 484	3 465 399	71.2	3 112 200	89.8

Source: General State Accounts (several years) and Budget Execution Report, fourth quarter 2009

5.6 ICT in higher education

Mozambique has made considerable progress in ICT development in higher education. Access to the internet and telecommunications in Mozambique has grown considerably, particularly due to the liberalisation of internet service providers (ISPs) and telecommunications services. From the early stages, the Centre for Informatics of the Eduardo Mondlane University (CIUEM) has been at the forefront of internet activities in Mozambique when it began to offer nationwide email services in the early 1990s (Mário *et al.* 2003). In 1996 Mozambique became the second country in sub-Saharan Africa (after South Africa) to achieve full internet connectivity through a dial-up connection between CIUEM and Rhodes University in South Africa. Although there are now several commercial ISPs in Mozambique, UEM remains the leader in internet development and information society initiatives in the country (Langa 2007).

CIUEM, a technical unit responsible for the development of ICT policies and operations at UEM, was established in 1979. In 1982, it became a formal computer centre, but also explored research issues around soft computer science and informatics. The centre also functions commercially, providing internet services, training, software, analysis and design, web design and hosting for private clients as well as the university (Ismail 2001). CIUEM provides access to a variety of stakeholders, including students, academic staff, government and business.

5.6.1   Second-generation providers

Internet usage in Mozambique has increased considerably, and promises to double annually for the foreseeable future. With the improvement in bandwidth and telecommunication infrastructure and the expansion of ISPs throughout the country, it is expected that such usage will expand considerably. However, the available bandwidth no longer satisfies the needs of individual users, businesses and any other entities in Maputo that receive services from the ISPs. While efforts should be made to improve the bandwidth to at least a 1 Mbps full-duplex link (i.e. 1 Mbps for uplink and downlink), most ISPs are only able to provide stable uplinks at 64 Kbps, with similar downlink speeds. The number of leased lines is also on an upward trend; but, even with innovative telecommunication pricing and internet policies, the price of access calls is still prohibitive throughout Mozambique (Langa 2007).

When the provision of email and internet services was initiated by CIUEM, it was the result of two years of intensive research activity on appropriate technologies and staff training, as well as the establishment of partnership agreements in the region. In 1997, through the Leland Initiative, USAID supported the establishment of five new ISPs, sharing a 128 Kbps gateway hosted by the Mozambican Telecommunication Company (TDM).

There are currently more than ten ISPs in Mozambique, but only Teledata and TDM have a point of presence (PoP) outside Maputo. In 2007, the total number of email users in the country was estimated at about 60 000, with more than 50% of which are based in Maputo. It would appear that high subscription fees limit the number of email subscribers. On average, most ISPs charge between USD 30 and USD 40 per month. At USD 25 per month, CIUEM offers one of the cheapest rates in the country. CIUEM administers the country's top-level domain, 'mz'. There were about 2 000 registered domains in different categories (SCAN-ICT 2002, Langa 2007).

5.6.2   Variables affecting ICT-enabled education

Variables	Enabling	Constraining
Policy framework and implementation	Mozambique has a national ICT policy that incorporates the education sector; a dedicated national ICT Policy Commission; and an implementation strategy.	
Infrastructure and access	Infrastructure and access have improved since the adoption of the national policy.	Infrastructure and access remain weak and largely confined to Maputo.
Collaborating mechanisms	The ICT Policy Commission's role is to encourage collaboration across the different ministries as well as with the private, civil society and donor sectors.	
Human resources capacity	The establishment of MICTI serves to address the long-term and strategic development of human resources capacity in ICTs in Mozambique.	There remains a very limited layer of skilled personnel and champions at national level, concentrated around a network of skilled engineers and personnel developed at the CIEUM.
Fiscal resources		The budget for the implementation of ICT programmes in Mozambique remains largely dependent on donor and private sector funding.
Learning content		Local, contextually relevant learning content is currently lacking, although there have been attempts at localising content produced in Brazil. The e-learning environment and use of ICT in teaching and learning is still far from ideal.
Procurement regulations		Duties and taxes currently levied on ICT products make them too expensive.
Attitudes	Within government leadership, there is a strong and positive attitude in favour of the promotion of ICTs for development, in general, and in education, in particular.	

Source: Maganlal 2007, Langa 2007

REFERENCES

Beverwijk J (2005) *The Genesis of a System: A coalition formation in Mozambican higher education*, 1993–2003. CHEPS/University of Twente.

Chilundo A (2010) Mozambique. In Pillay P (ed) *Higher Education Financing in East and Southern Africa*. Cape Town: African Minds.

Dias de Conceição MCL (1998) *Quality Management in Higher Education in Mozambique*. Bangor: University of Wales.

Direcção para a Coordenação do Ensino Superior (2009) *Estatísticas do Ensino Superior*. MEC: Maputo.

Gonçalves ACP (2007) A Concepção de Politecnia em Moçambique: Contradições de um discurso socialista (1983–1992) *Educação e Pesquisa*. São Paulo: Universidade Federal de Minas Gerais, 33(3): 601–619.

IMF (2012) *International Monetary Fund:* Mozambique. Available at: http://www.imf.org/external/pubs/ft/fandd/2006/03/country.htm [accessed 24 April 2012].

INE-MOZ (2012) *Instituto Nacional de Estatística*. Available at: www.ine.gov.mz [accessed 24 April 2012].

Ismail M (2001) Mozambique e-ready? Unpublished report. Information Technologies Group.

Johnstone D and Marcucci (2010) *Financing Higher Education Worldwide: Who Pays? Who Should Pay?* Baltimore: The John Hopkins University Press.

Langa P (2010) *Poverty Fighters in Academia: The Subversion of the Notion of Socially Engaged Science in Mozambican Higher Education*. Institute of Sociology Academia Sinica and the National Associations Liaison Committee of the ISA.

Langa P (2007) Mozambique. In: *ICTs and Higher Education in Africa: Status reports on information and communication technologies (ICTs) in higher education in eight African countries*. Cape Town: University of Cape Town.

Langa P (2006) The Constitution of the Field of Higher Education Institution in Mozambique. Unpublished Master's Dissertation. Cape Town: University of Cape Town Library.

Maganlal K (2007) ICT4Africa/Country Report Mozambique. Available at: http://www.wikieducator.org/ICT4Africa/Country_Report_Mozambique#ENABLING_AND_CONSTRAINING_FACTORS [accessed March 18 2007].

Mário M, Fry P, Lisbeth L and Chilundo A (2003) *Higher Education in Mozambique*. Oxford: James Currey.

MESCT (2003) *Nova Lei do Ensino Superior*. Maputo: República de Moçambique.

MINED (2012) *Plano Estratégico do Ensino Superior 2012–2020*. Maputo: DICES.

Taimo JU (2010) Ensino Superior em Moçambique: História, política e gestão. Unpublished doctoral dissertation. São Paulo: Universidade Metodista de Piracicaba.

Teixeira NP, Johnstone DB, Rosa MJ and Vossensteyn (2006) (eds) *Co-sharing and Accessibility in Higher Education: A fairer deal?* Dordrecht: Springer.

UNDP (2011) Human Development Index and Its Components. Available at: http://hdr.undp.org/en/media/HDR_2011_EN_Table1.pdf [accessed April 2012].

SÃO TOMÉ AND PRÍNCIPE

6.1   Country profile

São Tomé and Príncipe, officially the Democratic Republic of São Tomé and Príncipe, is a Portuguese-speaking island nation in the Gulf of Guinea, off the western equatorial coast of Central Africa. With an area of 1 001 square km and an estimated population of 175 000 inhabitants, the major challenge facing the country has been sustainable development in areas such as health, education, agriculture and infrastructure. São Tomé and Príncipe (STP) became independent from Portugal on 12 July 1975. Since independence, the country has evolved from a one party, socialist state to a liberal, multi-party democracy.

Constitutionally, the country is a semi-presidential republic: the president is the head of state and the prime minister the head of government. The current president is Manuel Pinto da Costa and the prime minister is Patrício Trovoada, the son of the former president Miguel Trovoada. In 2009, the Freedom House report ranked STP sixth in Africa in terms of civil liberties and political rights, and in 2011, STP scored 2 out of 7 (1 being the highest) in both of these categories. Freedom of the press is respected, and there are several independent newspapers (AEO 2012).

The free and transparent presidential elections of July 2011 (with a run-off in August) demonstrated the country's progress in consolidating stability. The second round was won by Manuel Pinto da Costa, STP's first post-independence president (from 1975 to 1991), who ran against the speaker of parliament, Evaristo de Carvalho. The political outlook for 2012 and 2013, however, is a matter of concern. Collaboration between the president and Prime Minister Patrício Trovoada has proven to be a challenge, and constitutes a significant risk for social stability (AEO 2012). Prime Minister Trovoada barely managed to pass the 2012 budget, and his government may find itself in a vulnerable position as it lacks a parliamentary majority.

São Tomé and Príncipe's literacy rate is around 84.4%. The youth population (15–24 years) has a higher literacy rate (93.8%). The age range of 22–24 years has a literacy rate of 94.7%, and literacy rates for the cohorts 15–16 and 20–21 years are 94.3% and 92.3% respectively (INE/QUIBB 2005). Portuguese is the official language of the country; the other widely spoken languages are *Forro, Angolar* and *Principense.*

In 2010 the country's main social indicators were as follows: life expectancy: 87.9 years (UNDP 2010); literacy rate, 68.3% (UNDP 2009); HDI: 0. 488 (130 in a list of 192 countries). According to the IMF (2012), the island's economic performance in 2011 was good despite a challenging external environment. The country is considered a fragile state according to the harmonised African Development Bank (AfDB) and World Bank Country Policy and Institutional Assessment (CPIA) score, which was below 3.2 in 2010. Its vulnerability to exogenous shocks is accompanied by high dependence on agriculture and overseas development assistance (ODA). In 2011 real GDP growth is estimated to have dropped slightly to 4.3% (down from 4.5% in 2010) and was driven mainly by the construction, consumer, retail, tourism and mining sectors. The service sector dominates the economy, accounting for about 60% of GDP in 2010 and 48.6% in 2011 and employing nearly 60% of the workforce. The industrial and agricultural sectors each contributed 20% to GDP (AEO 2012). The country imports some of its food, given that domestic food-crop production is not enough to meet local consumption. Other than agriculture, the main economic activities are fishing and a small industrial sector engaged in processing local agricultural products and producing a few basic consumer goods. The picturesque islands have great potential for tourism, and the government is attempting to improve its rudimentary tourist industry infrastructure. Since 2009 the government has made significant progress in reforming the management of public finances. The measures implemented have led the country to be ranked 12th out of 53 countries in the 2011 Ibrahim Index of African Governance (Ibrahim 2012).

6.2   Background and historical context of higher education

Higher education in São Tomé and Príncipe was established in the early 1990s. In 1975, when the country became independent, no HEI existed on the islands. From 1975 to the mid-1990s higher education could only be acquired overseas, mainly in Portugal and in the then-socialist countries. In 1994 the first HEI was established, the School of Accounting, Business Administration and Computing (IUCAI). IUCAI is a private institution (Lúcio 2012, interview).

Two years later, in 1996, the first public HEI, the Polytechnic Institute, was established and opened its gates in the academic year 1997/1998. By the mid-2000s, these two institutions were still the sole HEIs in the country, until the Portuguese Grupo Lusíada created the Universidade Lusíada de São Tomé e Príncipe in 2005.

6.3   Trends of expansion, diversity and differentiation

It is difficult to accurately map HEIs in São Tomé and Príncipe because of inconsistency in the data with respect to significant features and trends, along with related problems of data availability. The ministry of education does not have an institutional culture of gathering statistical data on higher education. The report presented here is therefore incomplete. It is based on primary sources obtained through interviews with key informants and the few available papers written on the country's higher education.

In 2012 São Tomé and Príncipe had three HEIs: two private and one public institution. As mentioned above, the Instituto Universitário de Contabilidade, Administração e Informática (IUCAI), was the first private HEI to be established in 1994. In 1996, the government established the Instituto Superior Politécnico (ISP), making it the sole public institutionm and in 2005, the Universidade Lusíada de São Tomé e Príncipe (ULSTP) was founded as the first fully fledged university in the country.

Table 6.1 Higher education institutions in São Tomé and Príncipe (2012)

| Year | Institution | Category | | | |
		Public	Annual fees	Private	Annual fee
1994	Instituto Universitário de Contabilidade, Administração e Informática (IUCAI)			X	95 Euro
1996	Instituto Superior Politécnico (ISP)	X	82 Euro		
2005	Universidade Lusíada De São Tomé e Príncipe (ULSTP)			X	75 Euro

Source: Author's field work 2012

IUCAI's Graduate Institute of Accounting, Business Administration and Computing thus emerged as the first institution of higher education in August 1994 by order No. 8/94 operating as a private institution. This private initiative resulted from an act in 1993 on the law of private and cooperative education (Law, 11/93). In Article 32, Law 11/93 allows other entities other than the state to operate higher education service providers.

By enacting this law the state aims to regulate the establishment of private education by recognising the universal right to high quality learning and teaching. However, the state continues to play a critical role in providing higher education to its citizens.

Table 6.2 below shows the evolution of enrolments in STP HE starting from the academic year 2000/2001, both in public and private institutions. Initially, private institutions did not keep enrolment records. The figures begin to appear in the academic year 2007/2008 with 558 enrolled students. The only public institution, the ISP, has kept enrolment records since 2000. Currently, there are more students in the two private institutions (1 050) than in the public institution (771). As we can read from these figures, higher education in STP is a young and very small system.

6.3.1 Students in the higher education system

Table 6.2 shows the evolution of the student population from the year 2002 to 2012. It was not possible to obtain data for the years 2000 to 2007/2008 for the private institutions.

Table 6.2 Student enrolment 2000–2012

Year	Number of students	
	Public institutions	Private institutions
	ISP	LUSTP e UICAI
2000/2001	55	No data
2001/2002	247	No data
2002/2003	317	No data
2003/2004	358	No data
2004/2005	427	No data
2005/2006	474	No data
2006/2007	539	No data
2007/2008	604	558
2008/2009	704	670
2009/2010	766	782
2010/2011	643	789
2011/2012	771	1 050

Source: Author's field work 2012

6.3.2 Academic programmes

Data concerning the academic programmes offered by the HEIs in São Tomé and Príncipe shows that the Instituto Superior Politécnico offers Bachelors degrees in several academic disciplines, such as Portuguese, French, mathematics, biology and history. The IUCAI mainly offers Bachelors degrees in business-oriented academic programmes: management, accounting, taxation and auditing, law, petrol management and economics, telecommunications and computer science engineering, law, civil engineering and tourism.

The Universidade Lusíada de São Tomé e Príncipe is also a business-oriented institution: it offers degrees in law, economics, business sciences and computer science. It was impossible to obtain data on the academic programmes offered by the fourth university, Universidade Lusófona de São Tomé e Príncipe (Pontifice 2003, Cardoso 2004). Moreover, data on the academic programmes offered by the other three HEIs presented above is likely to be incomplete and not updated. The field work research helped somewhat in obtaining systematised and updated data on higher education in São Tomé and Príncipe, mainly concerning enrolment trends in each HEIs from 1994 up to date, academic programmes and degrees offered since establishment and tuitions fees for each institution (see Table 6.1).

6.3.3 Academic degrees and diplomas

Law 2/2003 Art 13 prescribes the academic degrees and diplomas offered by HEIs in São Tomé and Príncipe.

- Universities can offer the academic degrees of Bacharelato, Licenciatura (Bachelors degree and Bachelor Honours degree), Masters and Doctorate;
- Polytechnics can offer *bacharelatos* and *licenciatura* degrees;
- Courses leading to *bacharelato* and *licenciatura* must have the normal length of three years, but in special cases, the duration can be of one or two semesters; and
- Courses leading to the academic degree of *Licenciatura* must have a duration of five years.

6.4   Changes in higher education governance

São Tomé and Principe does not have a specific higher education law. Higher education issues are legislated in the general law of education, Decree Law 2/2003, approved on 2 June 2003. In the section concerning higher education (subsection III, Articles 11, 12, 13, 14 and 15), Decree Law 2/2003 defines the scope and objectives, the academic degrees and the different kinds of HEIs. The objectives and academic degrees defined in the law are similar to the ones prescribed in the other Lusophone countries.

It is however worth mentioning that the law divides higher education into university and polytechnic training. University training is more academic, scientific and culturally-oriented than the polytechnic training, which is more concerned with professional and technical training. University training is offered at universities, whereas polytechnic training is offered at vocational or technical institutions.

The higher education system is supervised by the directorate of higher education and training, an institution integrated in the ministry of education, culture and training. Specific detail on how this board regulates and supervises higher education in the country, or concerning their vision and strategic plans, is unavailable.

6.5   Financing higher education

São Tomé and Príncipe has no clear funding policy for higher education, apart from the money that is allocated to scholarships for overseas studies. Over the past few years the government has kept overall public spending in the education sector (including capital expenditures) at about 10% of total government spending. While this allocation remains in line with the poverty reduction strategy on the island (PRSP), recurrent spending tends to favour higher education (currently at more than half of the sector's recurrent spending), mainly to pay for scholarships for students to study abroad (IMF 2008).

According to the IMF report, an alternative strategy to finance higher education in the country would also help to better balance financing primary and secondary education. Moreover, there are reports that suggest a higher level of corruption in the scholarship scheme. According to Vincente (2007) scholarships for higher education abroad have been a key source of social status for elite families. São Tomé and Príncipe relies exclusively on scholarships to study abroad, offered by foreign donors. Interestingly, that has been the primary way to educate the political elite in the country since gaining independence from Portugal.

In 2010, the Universidade Lusíada de São Tomé e Príncipe organised and hosted the second higher education forum in the country. The first forum had also been organised by ULSTP in 2006 under the theme 'Higher Education and Development'. The second forum discussed among other issues the funding in higher education, divided in three themes:

- Viability of funding for higher education;
- The role of the state in financing higher education; and
- Public-private partnership in higher education funding.

No official document or report was produced after the conference. From the five page memo it is possible to conclude that the issue of clarifying the scholarship allocation criteria is paramount. We can also deduce from the document that some of the participants were pushing for the introduction of a cost-sharing policy even for the beneficiaries of scholarships. The idea is that the beneficiaries of government scholarships should pay them back once they graduate and get a job. The money from the payments could be used to sponsor other students. None of this, however, was systematically documented apart from the small memo compiled by the secretariat of the conference.

6.6 ICT in higher education

ICT in São Tomé and Príncipe can best be characterised as poor and inadequate. According to a survey of ICT in education in Africa report (Fall 2007), the government does not consider ICT to be a priority sector, and there is currently no specific policy that addresses ICT. Internet service has not yet been liberalised, but there is some restructuring of the telecommunications sector underway. Other than basic computer facilities at the Polytechnic, it is not currently possible to identify any ICT initiatives in the country at any educational level.

The World Bank is pushing for the telecommunication market, currently a monopoly by Companhia São Tomense de Telecomunicação (CST) to be liberalised in order to increase efficiency and dynamism. After expanding by 60% in 2009, STP's mobile phone market grew by another 25% in 2010. With 100 000 mobile subscribers, market penetration stands at 60%. The country's connection to a marine fibre optic cable linking Africa's west coast to Europe, expected in 2012, should drastically improve telecommunications in the country. CST announced the conclusion of the USD 25 million contracts in June 2010. The project will be jointly financed by CST, the World Bank and Portugal Telecom. Once the cable is operational, CST plans to launch third-generation communication services (AEO 2012).

REFERENCES

AEO (2012) *Africa Economic Outlook. São Tomé and Príncipe.* Available at: http://www. africaneconomicoutlook.org/en/countries/west-africa/sao-tome-principe/ [accessed April 2012].

Agyeman OT (2007) *ICT in Education in São Tomé and Príncipe.* Available at: http://ddp-ext.worldbank.org/EdStats/GNBpro07.pdf [accessed April 2012].

Cardoso MM (2004) *Educação, Formação e Investigação em São Tomé e Príncipe: Será uma aposta do país no caminho para o desenvolvimento?* Paper presented on "VIII Congresso Luso-Africano-Brasileiro de Ciências Sociais", Centro de Estudos Sociais, Faculdade de Economia, Universidade de Coimbra. Lisboa: CEA/ISCTE. Available at: http://www.ces. uc.pt/lab2004/pdfs/MariaManuelaCardoso.pdf [accessed 23 August 2011].

Fall B (2007) *ICT in Education in São Tomé and Príncipe. Survey of ICT and education in Africa: São Tomé and Príncipe Country Report.* Available at: http://www.infodev.org/en/ publication.424.html [accessed April 2012].

IMF (2012) *IMF Mission to the Democratic Republic of São Tomé and Príncipe Reaches Staff-Level Agreement on US$3.97 Million ECF-Supported Programme.* Available at: http://www.imf.org/external/np/sec/pr/2012/pr12182.htm (accessed May 2012].

IMF (2008) *São Tomé and Príncipe: Poverty reduction strategy paper progress report.* Washington DC: International Monetary Fund.

Instituto Nacional de Estatística/QUIBB (2005) Alfabetização. Available at: http://www.ine. st/educacao/alfabetizacao.htm [accessed April 2012].

Lei 11/90. Lei do Ensino Particular e Cooperativo. 4º Sumplemento. Diário da Republica. São Tomé e Príncipe.

Mo-Ibrahim Foundation (2012) 2011 Ibrahim índex of African Governance. Available at: http://www.moibrahimfoundation.org/en/media/get/20111003_ENG2011-IIAG-SummaryReport-sml.pdf [accessed June 2012].

Pontifice, MF (n/d) *Educação Superior em São Tomé e Príncipe.* Seminário Internacional Educação Superior na CPLP/PUCRS. Available at: http://www.pucrs.br/edipucrs/cplp/ arquivos/pontifice.pdf [accessed 23 August 2011].

UNDP (2010) *Human Development Index.* Available at: http://hdr.undp.org/en/media/Lets-Talk-HD-HDI_2010.pdf [accessed 23 August 2011].

Interviews

Mr Lucio Pinto. Interview 24 February 2012

Alzira Rodrigues

Maria Fernanda Pontifice

CHAPTER

7

CONCLUSION

This study looked at the manner in which higher education in the Portuguese speaking countries in Africa developed, from its conception to today. This chapter sums up the study, and presents the various conclusions arrived at in the preceding chapters.

The study has shown that higher education in the five PALOP countries took different trajectories, in some cases with similarities, in terms of its formation and development. While Angola and Mozambique saw their first HEIs being established during the colonial period, to meet the demands and interests of the colonial settler populations, higher education in Cape Verde, Guinea-Bissau and São Tomé and Príncipe is a postcolonial experience.

In the postcolonial era, all five countries attempted to build socialist societies. The bi-polarisation of the international political order which led to the Cold War served as the ideological background behind the civil wars in Angola and Mozambique. The wars in Angola and Mozambique lasted more than 20 years and paralysed the two countries economically, bringing them almost to the brink of collapse. While Cape Verde and São Tomé and Príncipe remained politically calm, Guinea-Bissau has never enjoyed an enduring peace in its political process since gaining independence from Portugal in 1974. Consecutive *coups d'état* make the news headlines of the Guinea-Bissau political system.

In the mid-1980s, after their failed socialist experiment, all five countries joined the Breton Woods institutions, the IMF and the World Bank, and endured the necessary structural adjustment policies to revitalise their respective under-performing economies. Most sectors of the economy and services were liberalised.

The liberalisation of these countries' economies brought about many changes, some of which impacted drastically on higher education. The state could no longer afford to be the sole provider of higher education and it made space for private operators. In the mid-1990s the number of HEIs in Angola and Mozambique began to increase, with the emergence of private providers. Cape Verde, Guinea-Bissau, and São Tomé and Príncipe saw their first HEIs being established by private providers. The trend of expansion, differentiation and diversification has continued to date.

In all five countries, the first decade of the 21st century has been marked by an increasing participation in higher education even though the rates are still below the African average of 6.8% gross enrolment rate (GER). Cape Verde makes the exception with a participation rate of 22%, being amongst the highest on the continent, with Mauritius leading with 37% GER. The trends of expansion, differentiation and diversification of the higher education system in the PALOP are quite similar. However, each country is at a different stage of development of its higher education system.

While Angola and Mozambique have relatively large and complex systems with more than 100 000 students, distributed across the various public and private institutions, Cape Verde, Guinea-Bissau, and São Tomé and Príncipe are small systems, with fewer than 10 000 students mostly distributed in one major public institution and a few private operators.

The five countries have also experienced changes in the manner in which their higher education systems are governed. From a centralised and planning mode of governance and coordination during the socialist experiment, government being the sole provider of higher education, they have moved into a somewhat decentralised mode of governance with the government playing a regulatory role through passing public policy and regulations and the establishment of councils with a coordinating role.

The five countries present different higher education governing structures. Currently, Angolan higher education is governed and coordinated by the ministry of higher education, science and technology, and it also has a secretariat of state for the sector. Cape Verde has a ministry of higher education, science and innovation. These two are somewhat autonomous ministries, separated from the ministry of education. Mozambique initially established a ministry of higher education, science and technology, but in 2005 science and technology became a ministry on its own, while higher education was relegated to a general directorate within the ministry of education and culture. Guinea-Bissau and São Tomé and Príncipe also have general directorates for higher education within the ministry of education.

External quality assurance (QA) is a recent phenomenon in Africa and in the PALOP countries in particular. PALOP countries have experienced a significant increase in the number of students participating in higher education. That came along with an increase in the number of both public and private providers. QA emerged as a response to the growing public perception that the quality of higher education is being compromised in the effort to increase enrolments, particularly through privatisation. The PALOP countries are at different stages of establishing QA systems. Mozambique and Angola already have QA agencies, while Cape Verde is in the process of preparing the relevant legislation to introduce QA mechanisms. Guinea-Bissau, and São Tomé and Príncipe are lagging behind in this regard. There have however been debates in these countries about the need to establish quality assurance mechanisms for their higher education systems.

Higher education financing in the five case studies varies considerably. Generally, public funding of higher education in these countries is constrained, and governments have been contemplating various cost sharing mechanisms. In Angola, the financial resources of higher education are obtained mainly from four sources: the state budget, student fees, contributions from private and international donors, and paid services to individual or corporate users.

The higher education public sector is predominantly financed by the state budget. Private HEIs depend mainly on tuition fees and other fees paid by students.

In Cape Verde, there are two mechanisms of financing higher education, namely public and private financing. While public financing is mainly through state appropriations, private financing is mainly through fees paid by students.

Public institutions in Mozambican higher education are funded from four different sources: government funding, donor support, student fees, and income generating activities. The government's budget is the public institutions' largest source of revenue. About 97% of public institutions' budget is supported by the government and each institution negotiates its budget directly with the ministry of finance. Donor support takes different forms, including scholarships and training opportunities, technical assistance, research support and capacity building. Student fees are also another source of revenue for public institutions, but their amount is negligible. Mozambique is currently working towards the introduction of a cost-sharing model to finance higher education.

Like many other African countries, Guinea-Bissau faces inadequate public financing, and the share of private resources in higher education financing is expanding. The contribution from households accounts for approximately 50% of national expenditure (state and households) on higher education.

São Tomé and Príncipe has no clear funding policy for higher education, apart from the money that is allocated to scholarships abroad. Over the past few years, the government has kept overall public spending in the education sector (including capital expenditures) at about 10% of total government spending.

ICT infrastructure in the PALOP higher education arena can best be described as improving in Angola, Cape Verde and Mozambique, and challenging in Guinea-Bissau and São Tomé and Príncipe. Angola, Cape Verde and Mozambique are making considerable strides towards expanding access to the internet and computer labs, particularly in the public institutions. The three countries have comprehensive national ICT policies. The situation is different in Guinea-Bissau, and São Tomé and Príncipe, where the ICT infrastructure remains under-developed.

Appendix 1

Building a higher education research network and advocacy for the PALOP: HERANA-PALOP

Building prosperity in these challenging times requires that nations reach out beyond their borders, more than ever before, to establish strategic international connections. Increasingly, the right doors are being opened and the path to prosperity is being constructed through partnerships being forged by universities in research, innovation and higher education.[1]

1   Introduction

The idea of undertaking a study that maps the state of higher education in the five Portuguese Speaking Countries in Africa (PALOP) was to bring higher education in these countries into the spotlight, since historically they have been neglected from the mainstream of higher education research, policy and advocacy in Africa. There is a significant amount of research on Anglophone and Francophone higher education in Africa compared to the insufficient research on PALOP. ADEA's initiative to support this study is therefore an unprecedented effort which should be commended and encouraged.

The aim of the appendix to this report is to present preliminary results of the advocacy work undertaken in PALOP to support a more integrated higher education research network in PALOP. I discuss ideas and proposals gathered from different stakeholders.

The ideas gathered from these sources could serve as the basis to build a sustainable higher education research and advocacy network amongst PALOP and between PALOP and other networks, such as the Higher Education Research and Advocacy Network in Africa (HERANA).[2]

---

1   Toope, S (2012) *Building prosperity through higher education connections with Brazil.* Online. Available: http://www.universityworldnews.com/article.php?story=20120515124848851.
2   http://chet.org.za/programmes/herana/

2 Bringing PALOP into HERANA

2.1 About HERANA

HERANA is an expertise network aimed at developing higher education studies and research in Africa, coordinated by the Centre for Higher Education Transformation (CHET) in Cape Town, South Africa. The *University World News[3]* is a partner in this project helping to disseminate its activities. The research component of HERANA is investigating the complex relationships between higher education and development in the African context, with a specific focus on economic and democratic development. A new research area is exploring the use of research in policy-making. HERANA has established two research information distribution portals. The HERANA Gateway is being developed to distribute research-based information to relevant experts and decision-makers. The Gateway is already operational at www.herana-gateway.org. It uses a dedicated Google box to search the websites of a number of organisations that store publications and reports on higher education in Africa.

Mozambique is the sole country involved regularly in the HERANA projects. The country has been benefiting from useful data produced under the studies conducted by different experts linked to the HERANA network. On the one hand, during this study, I contacted various key players in PALOP about the idea of developing a similar HERANA–PALOP NETWORK project for the five Portuguese countries.

This idea was overwhelmingly welcomed, and most of the people I approached are in top managerial positions in their respective countries (see the List of Interviews on page xii). With the necessary support from ADEA or any other agency it would be possible to develop a network of higher education researchers for PALOP. On the other hand, since Mozambique and Eduardo Mondlane University are well connected to HERANA, it would be possible to link the two projects.

Regarding further initiatives for the advancement of higher education in the, it is strongly recommended to:

- Map the existing research expertise in the field.
- Track and promote forms of aid to higher education in PALOP.
- Systematically collect a variety of data on higher education, and develop a database on the basis of performance indicators that can be utilised by, amongst others, institutional leaders, funders and governments in making evidence-based knowledge policy decisions about higher education.
- Establish an observatory for higher education to monitor the development of higher education in PALOP and link it to the African Union's Education Observatory which receives significant technical support from ADEA's Working Group on Education Management and Policy Support (WGEMPS) based in Harare, Zimbabwe.
- In doing the above, to solicit the support of ADEA's WGEMPS and WGHE.

---

3   http://www.universityworldnews.com/

3   Masters programme in higher education

The Masters programme in higher education studies and development (MHESD) is a collaborative programme involving the Eduardo Mondlane University (UEM, Mozambique), the University of Oslo (Norway), the University of the Western Cape (UWC, South Africa), the Centre for Higher Education studies and Development (CESD, Mozambique) and the Centre for Higher Education Transformation (CHET, South Africa). The author of this report, Dr Patrício Langa, was instrumental in the establishment of the MHESD programme at the Faculty of Education of Eduardo Mondlane and bringing in the collaborative partners from South Africa and Norway.

MHESD at UEM is a coursework-based programme focusing on the changing functions, policies and operations of higher education in Africa. Before engaging in the thesis research, students take a number of coursework modules, viz. Introduction to Higher Education (taught to some students at the University of Oslo as part of the Erasmus Mundus European Masters in Higher Education Programme and quota scholarship scheme); Research Methods and Proposal Development; and Higher Education and Development (to be taught at UWC); and the remaining modules taken in Maputo. Through various disciplinary perspectives, the programme provides students with a solid basis for analysing and critically assessing change processes at all relevant levels in higher education and development. This Masters programme is the first of its kind to be established in Mozambique. The programme focuses on the complex relationship between higher education and development, particularly in sub-Saharan African countries. The programme is linked to a research network on expertise in higher education in Africa (HERANA), giving successful applicants access to the latest knowledge in the field.

3.1   Developing an academic exchange programme

During the visit to PALOP, I contacted various academics and higher education officials from the ministries. All those contacted were extremely interested in the idea of developing an academic exchange programme involving students and academic staff from the PALOP (see List of Interviews on page 103). The universities of PALOP would have an opportunity to use the new Masters programme in Maputo, the first of its kind in PALOP, as the starting point to train the much needed breed of experts in higher education studies and development for their respective countries.

All director generals of higher education and institutional leaders support this idea. The next step to take advantage of this opportunity would be to identify potential funders for the project, provided that a higher education working group made up of at least five members (one from each country) could be established and present a project. Once again, ADEA could play a critical role in the implementation of this initiative.

Reputable personalities such as Prof. Victor Kajibanga and Paulo de Carvalho from Agostinho Neto University, Angola; Claudio Furtado, Tolentino Cursino, the current minister of higher education, science and innovation, António Correia, Cape Verde, Rui

Ladim, current president of the installation committee of Amílcar Cabral's University, João Ribeiro Butiam Có, the current director general of higher education, Guinea-Bissau; Fernanda Pontifice, former minister of education, São Tomé and Príncipe, to mention some, are available and eager to contribute to the implementation of such an initiative.

4 Association of Portuguese speaking universities (AULP)

AULP[4], the Association of Portuguese Speaking Universities, has as its objective to promote cooperation between higher education and research institutions by means of exchange of students, professors and researchers, and of participation in research projects by sharing information. For more than 20 years, AULP has been striving to gain international recognition for the achievements of this Portuguese speaking community. Even though this association brings together other members who are not from the PALOP, it can be utilised as a platform to extend the PALOP network.

5 Revista Inter-universitária – PALOP (RIU–PALOP)

One of my responsibilities during the visit to the PALOP, apart from the baseline study, was to initiate contacts to set the stage for the establishment of a forum to facilitate networking among key actors in higher education in the PALOP in order to improve information flow, joint policy dialogue for sharing experiences of good practice and promising approaches: research, teaching, data and advocacy. This idea was discussed with the key participants in the study during the fieldwork visits. Most participants recommended the establishment of an academic journal that would enable regular exchange of information and an opportunity to publish the work of PALOP academics. Consensus was reached that the journal should cover three broad areas: education (higher), culture and society. The journal would be registered in Cape Verde (the registration process is in progress), and have an editorial board with members from the various PALOP universities. A proposal for the editorial board has already been established involving some of the people in the list of the academic personalities I interacted with during the visit to PALOP.

---

4   http://www.aulp.org/

Appendix 2

Interviews

ANGOLA

Prof. Adão do Nascimento – Scholar and secretary of state for higher education
Prof. Paulo de Carvalho – Faculty of Social Sciences, Agostinho Neto University
Prof. Victor Kajinbanga – Dean of the Faculty of Social Sciences, Agostinho Neto University
Dr   Eugénio Novais – National director for higher education development and expansion
Mr   Július Nierere de Campos e Almeida – Director of the minister's office (ministry for higher education, science and technology)
Mrs   Isabel Pinto – Research assistant
Mrs   Sónia Cassule – Education journalist, editor of *Caderno de emprego*

CAPE VERDE

Prof. Arlindo Mendes – Former coordinator of postgraduate studies
Dr   Amália Lopes – Former director general of higher education and science
Dr   André Corsino Tolentino – Former minister of education, diplomat, member of the Portuguese Academy of Science, former ambassador of Cape Verde in Portugal
Dr   António Leão de Aguiar Correia e Silva – Minister of higher education, science and innovation
Dr   Bartolomeu Varela – Former administrator and director of University of Cape Verde (UNI-CV), assistant professor of social sciences and humanities
Mr   Arnaldo Jorge Brito – Director general, directorate general of higher education
Mr   Crisanto Barros – Former vice-rector of UNI-CV and a member of the installation committee of UNI-CV
Mr   Emanuel Borges – Senior technician, planning and statistics, ministry of higher education, science and innovation

GUINEA-BISSAU

Mr Alfredo Gomes – Former minister of national education and higher education
Mr Delfim da Silva – Former minister of foreign affairs and former minister of education
Mr Jailson Cuino – Former director general of higher education, ministry of education
Mr João Ribeiro Butiam Có – Director general of higher education, ministry of education
Mr Mamadou Saliv Jassie – Former director general of higher education
Mr Mamadu Jao – Director of the national institution for studies and research
Mr Miguel de Barros – Sociologist, former research fellow of the INEP
Mr Rui Landim – President of the Commission for the Restoration of the University of Amílcar Cabral
Ms Lucy Monteiro – Sociologist, former lecturer, University Hills Boé
Mr Ivo de Barros – Lawyer

MOZAMBIQUE

Prof. Arlindo Chilundo – Deputy minister for higher education in the ministry of education
Dr Nelson Zavale – Research assistant, lecturer at the Faculty of Education of the Eduardo Mondlane University, Masters Programme in Higher Education Studies and Development
Mr Graciano Cumaio – Head of department of planning in the directorate for coordination of higher education, ministry of education
Mrs Denise Malawene – National director of the directorate for coordination of higher education
Ms Tania Ferreira – Research assistant and Masters student in Higher Education Studies and Development Programme, Faculty of Education of the Eduardo Mondlane University

SÃO TOMÉ AND PRÍNCIPE

Mr Lucio Pinto – Presidente of the Fundação ATENA, the entity that established the University Lusiadas (UNI-Lusiadas)
Ms Alzira Rodrigues – Former president of the Instituto Superior Politécnico, and coordinator for the installation of the University of São Tomé and Príncipe
Ms Maria Fernanda Pontifice – Former minister of education, rector of the University of Lusiadas

About the author

Patrício Vitorino Langa is assistant professor in the Faculty of Education at the Eduardo Mondlane University in Mozambique, where he coordinates *inter alia* the Masters programme in higher education studies and development (MHESD). Dr Langa is also a visiting research fellow at the University of the Western Cape (South Africa) where he was a post-doctoral research fellow in 2010 and 2011. He holds a PhD and a MEd in Sociology and Higher Education Studies from the University of Cape Town (UCT) and has a wide-ranging list of publications on sociology and higher education studies focusing on Africa and southern Africa more specifically. His recent publications include: Langa, P (2012) É possível ver de lugar nenhum?: Sobre o ponto de vista sociológico, *Botelin Científico Sapiens Research*, *2(1): 46–49*; Langa, P. (2011) The Significance of Bourdieu's Concept of Cultural Capital in Analysing the Field of Higher Education in Mozambique, *International Journal of Contemporary Sociology, Vol. 48(1): 93–116*; Wangenge-Ouma, G and Langa, P (2010) Universities and the Mobilization of Claims of Excellence for Competitive Advantage. *Higher Education, Vol. 59 (6): 749–764*. Dr Langa is the founder and Director of the Centre for Higher Education Studies and Development (CESD) in Maputo and the current president of the Mozambican Sociological Association (AMS). He is also the National Director for external evaluation in the National Council for Quality Assurance in Higher Education (CNAQ) and board member in the National Council of Higher Education (CNES) in Mozambique. His key research interests are in the areas of epistemology, sociology of (higher) education, social theory and higher education, higher education policy studies and higher education and development.